REVELATION AND DANIEL REVEAL

HOW AND WHEN THE WORLD ENDS

(Volume 4)

Earl Bristow

*To Dad,
Love,
Paula*

Copyright © 2020 Earl Bristow

All rights reserved. No part of this book may be reproduced or used in any manner without written permission of the copyright owner except for the use of quotations in a book review.

For more information:
Contact: erbrist@gmail.com

Scripture taken from the New King James Version®.Copyright © 1982 by Thomas Nelson. Used by permission. All rights reserved.

All scriptures quoted in this publication are quoted from the New King James Bible, unless otherwise noted.

DEDICATION

I wish to dedicate this book to the readers of my books. I have been humbled by the favorable reviews and comments about the books in this series. As a new author, the encouragement from the personal emails has been particularly rewarding. The emails and reviews were totally unexpected.

When the Holy Spirit began planting the seed for me to write a book, I laughed and thought it was a crazy passing thought. Frankly, I resisted for several months.

Finally, I began to see the light. God wanted me to share the HOPE of eternity that burns within my soul. My desire is for every person who reads these books to come away refreshed and full of HOPE.

Thank you again for your support. I speak blessing of HOPE and joy to you!

Earl Bristow

ACKNOWLEDGMENS

As a new author I am anxious to interact with my readers via email, so my email is placed at both the front and back of my books. It is gratifying to receive email asking for explanations on topics within the books. Some readers share other viewpoints and ask for my opinion. Several have become my new "internet friends."

One in particular has proven to be an invaluable contributor to my last book and this one, Gerald Collins.

When I prepared an outline for this book, several chapters on the Millennium and Eternity were planned. These are Bible topics I had never studied in-depth. They were part of my curriculum in Seminary and Bible college, but that was over thirty years ago. I needed help, so I asked Gerald to give me ideas.

Gerald has read countless numbers of End Time books, book marked more End Time internet web sites, and read more blogs from authors than anybody I know. He supplied me with so much data, it became apparent a separate book was needed to adequately cover these subjects.

If that was not enough, he agreed to proof areas in this book that are both controversial and difficult to explain in simple terms. With his help, hopefully _we_ have created a book that is easily read and with sound Biblical interpretations.

Thank you, Gerald, my friend. God bless you for helping spread the word – Jesus is coming!

Maranatha!!
Earl Bristow

Table of Contents

Dedication iii
Acknowledgmens iv

Chapter 1: Introduction 1
Chapter 2: Update on Current Signs 7
Chapter 3: God's Love and Master Plan 16
Chapter 4: God's Unfulfilled Promises 21
Chapter 5: The Mosaic Covenant & God Turns His Back on Israel ... 29
Chapter 6: Daniel's 70 Weeks Contain the Timeline for End Time Events 35
Chapter 7: Daniel, Matthew, and Revelation Part 1 The Dream 41
Chapter 8: Daniel, Matthew, and Revelation Part 2 Tribulation 57
Chapter 9: Daniel, Matthew, and Revelation – Part 3 The Coming Kingdom 64
Chapter 10: Revelation Summary 68
Chapter 11: Revelation – The Reasons for the Judgments 81
Chapter 12: The Jewish Feasts in End Times Events 91
Chapter 13: The Rapture and the Marriage Supper of the Lamb 97
Chapter 14: Judgment Seat of Christ or Bema Seat Judgment 107
Chapter 15: How and When the Tribulation Starts 109
Chapter 16: The Battle of Armageddon and Judgment 117
Chapter 17: Conclusion 127

Concluding Thoughts 131
A Thank You From The Author 134
Glossary of Terms 135
Bibliography 141

Chapter 1

Introduction

Heaven and Eternity - are they real?

Are Bible prophecies true and is the end of this age near?

Is there any hope for us?

As the days and years flow by and as we grow older, an increasing desire within us seeks to find out what our future holds. Anxieties arise concerning our journey through life.

> *Will I be successful?*
> *Will I marry and have a family?*
> *Will I be happy and content?*
> *Will I have enough money to provide peace and security in retirement?*

At some point in our lives, questions arise pertaining to God.

> *Is God real?*
> *Are Heaven and Hell real?*
> *Will there be a judgment of evil people?*

People who ask the above questions finally get to a very personal question, *"What will happen to me when I die?"*

> *Is death the end of everything, or is it only the beginning of the endless ages yet to come?*
>
> *If there is life after death, what will it be like?*

Answers to these eternal questions will be provided and discussed by providing a summary of the Rapture, The Tribulation, the Millennium, and Eternity. The descriptions originate primarily from Revelation, Daniel and Mathew 24. Some key discussions are:

- Prophecies about the Rapture and Tribulation.
- A description of the twenty one plagues occurring during the Tribulation.
- God's unfulfilled promises to Abraham, King David and Israel.
- A detailed study on the last three and one half years of the Tribulation.
- A description of the 1,000 years known as the Millennial Reign of Jesus.
- Participants in the Millennial Kingdom.

You will be presented with in-depth comparisons of the prophecies including descriptions of how they are interrelated to each other. When appropriate, similar prophecies from other books of the Bible will be inserted as well. This book will help you to see how committed God is to providing us with knowledge and understanding of future End Time events. At the conclusion of this study, you should have a better understanding of God's master plan for the redemption of humanity from sin and death.

We do not have to be unaware of the End Time events that are coming. If you fear the end of the world, knowledge will displace this fear. Understanding these events reveal a glorious reward awaiting believers when the next age for humanity begins, the Millennial Reign of Jesus.

End Time prophecies in the Bible have intrigued and fascinated multitudes of people throughout the centuries. More commentaries and books have been written and published about Revelation than any other book in the Bible. Many of these books propose different interpretations of identical scriptures about End Time prophecies. A large number of books are written on Daniel and the prophetic portions of Matthew 24, also offering differing interpretations of the same scriptures.

If you don't believe the amazing forecasts in Daniel, Revelation, Matthew, and multiple other minor prophetic books of the Bible will come to pass, please examine the record of *completed* Bible prophecy. Go to your computer, open Google, and type in fulfilled Bible prophecies. You will get so many hits you can spend days validating the truth of hundreds of Bible prophecies. Virtually all of these were long range prophecies. Many were not fulfilled for hundreds and some for several thousand years. Composing such projections were far beyond the abilities of man to make using analytical reasoning or by guessing.

Biblical prophecies are genuine and divinely inspired. They will be fulfilled. The book of Revelation is the final book in the Bible giving us a vision of the future. Therefore, it is a tremendously important book for every Christian to study and understand. The book of Revelation enables you to understand the coming Millennium and Eternity. It also brings to conclusion God's master plan of redemption for humanity from wickedness and sin.

Bible scholars describe God as omnipotent, omnipresent, and omniscient. Let me translate these into simple English.

- Omnipotent – God has unlimited power and He is able to do anything.
- Omnipresent – God can be present everywhere at the same time.
- Omniscient – God knows everything.

God is the supreme being of the universe because He created it. Since God created time, He stands outside of it and is able to see the end from the beginning.

> "*[10]I make known the end from the beginning, from ancient times, what is still to come." (Isaiah 46:10)*

Since God knows the ending of our current world and humanity, He has chosen to share some of His knowledge about the future.

To get a complete historical perspective of God's master plan and timeline for humanity, please consider reading the other books in the End of World Series. The background information in them will better facilitate your understanding of this book.

How and When the World Ends (Book 1) reveals the day (not the date or year) the Rapture will occur. *End Time Rapture Signs* (Book 2) provides a historical overview of the signs God has used throughout history to warn humanity judgment is coming. Then it transitions into current signs to watch for that signal the Rapture date is approaching. *The Date of the Rapture* (Book 3) discusses in detail the history of God's covenants and major paradigm shifts in God's plan. The covenants demonstrate God's relentless pursuit to redeem humanity from sin and they prepare the way for the last paradigm shift – the Rapture. Then the probable Rapture date and alternative dates are discussed.

God has a master plan to offer humanity redemption one last time. This occurs during the Tribulation before we enter into the next phase of our existence, the Millennial reign of Jesus. God reveals His plan through Bible prophecies, which brings us to the purpose of this book.

When God desires to emphasize something, He repeats it. One of my goals is to present the same prophecy from multiple sources in the Bible. God desires for believers to understand the End Times. Therefore, He repeats the same message using multiple prophets.

Most Christians don't understand why God's master plan includes the Tribulation. If asked to describe specifics about it, most will describe a vague concept that bad things happen during the Tribulation. If asked for examples, they will describe one or maybe two of these events: the four horsemen of the apocalypse, monsters attacking people, or giant bees with huge stingers. Most are unaware there are _no_ believers initially present during this time.

The Tribulation can be compared to a love story of a husband and wife. The faithful lover is God, who has tried numerous ways to get the lover back. The unfaithful lover is anyone who has chosen to follow their own desires and pleasures with other lovers. The desire to get the unfaithful lover back blocks out all the previous rejections, so one last chance to the unfaithful lover is extended before permanently ending the relationship.

Two parables from the Bible which illustrate this love story are the prodigal son and the lost sheep. The prodigal son asked his father for and received his half of his future inheritance. His brother remained and faithfully served his father. The prodigal son went out spent all of his inheritance on wild and immoral living. A severe famine occurred. The son was starving so he decided to go back to his father's house and ask to become one his servants so he would not starve. However, his father welcomed him back as a son, but he had lost his future inheritance (Luke 15:11-32). The parable illustrates it is never too late to come back to our heavenly Father.

Jesus also gave us the parable of the lost sheep to illustrate God's love. One sheep strayed from the flock. The shepherd left the flock of ninety-nine sheep to search for the one lost sheep to bring it home (Matthew 18:12-14). God will keep searching for every lost soul until the day they die.

God will use the seven years of Tribulation to offer all non-believing Gentiles, Jews, and the nation of Israel an opportunity to turn from their wicked ways and acknowledge Him as God.

NOTE: A Glossary of Terms at the end of this book is designed to help you with any terms you may not understand. Many people get confused over the beasts in Daniel versus the beasts in Revelation. The Glossary provides descriptions of the beasts, the ten horns, the false prophet and other terms that will assist you in understanding this book.

The following chapter is an update on the current End Time signs and world events of today.

Chapter 2

Update on Current Signs

This book was started in April 2020 while a stay at home order was in place due to the virus pandemic. Amazon instituted strict polices prohibiting books published after April 2020 from naming the pandemic virus ravaging the world. I respect their polices, so it will be referred to as *the virus* or *the pandemic virus* in this book. My heartfelt sympathy and prayers go out to the people who have lost loved ones.

The 2020 *virus pandemic* is an event unlike any event in modern history. It is also a warning sign from God to show us how vulnerable humanity is to one of the End Times signs, pestilence. There will be more signs coming, so don't be surprised when they occur.

The following summary was prepared on June 10, 2020 providing updates and future predictions for the impact of the *pandemic.* It has also created two new situations that impact the End Times which will be explained.

- Worldwide 405,000 have died and it is projected to increase to over 700,000 by the end of 2020. If accurate records become available, deaths easily exceed one million.

- The current U.S. death toll is 115,000. The projection for 2020 is that 175,000 to 200,000 will die.

- Approximately two-thirds of the U.S. population were ordered to stay at home or shelter in place during the month of April.
- People are being encouraged by the CDC to wear face masks when in public places while exercising social distancing by staying six feet apart from each other.
- Virtually all *non-essential* businesses nationwide were shut down until May 1, 2020.
- Starting in approximately mid-May, most states started reopening non-essential business with severe time-phased constraints, e.g., capacity at restaurants not to exceed 25% until the next phase if the virus does not spike when people begin interacting outside their home.
- The number of unemployed exceeded 30 million at the end of May (includes those on furlough due to virus).
- Over 100,000 U.S. small and medium size businesses are projected to fail and not reopen.
- Hundreds of thousands of jobs are permanently lost.
- The U.S. and global economy are projected to remain in a severe recession until the spring or summer of 2021.
- A new normal for social distancing and working online have changed work and shopping patterns permanently.
- Some churches reopened in May, but because of social distancing requirements, longer term attendance is projected to be down by 40 to 50%.
- Thousands of churches are projected to permanently close due to lack of finances.

The problems in many nations of the world are worse than the U.S. Many economists are predicting a global depression.

God has used *the virus* to put humanity on notice of their vulnerability. This pandemic is a major sign from God. Expect more warning signs to come.

Until a vaccine is developed, sickness and death will continue.

An unprecedented amount of research for a cure for the virus has resulted in promising new treatments. A couple of clinical labs are touting the possible availability by the fall of 2020 for these treatments. However, treatments only increase the survival rate and will not prevent people from contracting the virus.

To hasten the development of a vaccine to prevent the *virus*, President Trump established the project *Operation Warp Speed* to develop a vaccine in 2020 with a goal of making 100 million doses of vaccine available by November, 200 million by December, and 300 million by January, 2021.

A similar effort in 1976 to fight the swine flu failed. Insurers' and manufactures' concerns about liability issues forced Congress to pass a law waiving liability. This legislation slowed down the release of the vaccine. Near the completion of the vaccine, one side effect identified in 94 people was an immune system disease, Guillain-Barre syndrome. This shut the entire program down. The same type of obstacles could slow down the development of the vaccine for this virus.

Until a vaccine is available, the *pandemic virus* will be like a black cloud hanging over the world.

We will have to continue to cope with sickness and death. Mounting fears of insecurity and hopelessness abound worldwide. HOPE is essential for everyone's mental health, or fear and depression will control people's minds.

Many are seeking answers, but can't find them from government or media sources.

God provides *HOPE* to every believer! Believers will be spending the Millennium and Eternity with God in renewed bodies where pain and suffering are non-existent. During the Millennium, peace, happiness, and joy will abound.

While we live on earth, *you* should believe for the Rapture and that Jesus is coming *for you*. This is the *blessed hope* for which we should constantly watch for and pray to come to pass.

God is presenting sign after sign to demonstrate His power and humanity's vulnerability. However, most people are unprepared and many will miss the Rapture.

In Book 2, *End Time Rapture Signs*, signs to watch for were discussed, e.g., wars, rumors of war, famine, and pandemics, etc. We can't put God in the *proverbial box*, so we need to learn to recognize God's signs. The current *pandemic* discussed earlier is a major sign. More signs will follow.

Since its publication on March 28, 2020, two additional important signs have appeared. These are the oil crisis and China's aggressive move to dominate the world. Both will contribute to the collapse of the world's financial systems during the Tribulation. These are the types of events God uses to show believers who are watching that we are progressing closer and closer to the Rapture.

Oil

The pandemic has caused the global economy to slam on the brakes, leading to an extremely sharp drop in demand for oil. It has created a massive oil glut and raised concerns about the lack of physical storage space for it. On April 18, 2020, traders had an inventory of oil that had to be sold, but all storage facilities were full. There were no buyers among the distributors and refiners in the market place. Oil could not be given away for free. So, some traders who were desperate to get rid of inventory, began to pay as much as $37.63 per barrel to get anyone to accept delivery of their oil. Never has oil fallen below zero and never have sellers had to pay buyers to take oil inventories.

The dramatic price decrease from $55 per barrel in February 2020 to $25 on May 3, 2020 has caused significant harm to the economies of countries that rely on oil for most of their cash income. These countries are significant players in the End Times: Russia, Saudi Arabia, and Libya. The longer term effect of diminished cash results in decreased stability with increasing volatility in these nations. Seeds are being sown for further escalation of conflict and unrest in the Middle East.

China

The following article from Forbes dated May 4, 2020 sums up known facts revealed by the U.S. Department of Homeland Security about China's involvement in the *pandemic*:

China Covered Up *Virus* To Hoard Medical Supplies, DHS Report Finds

By Isabel Togoh

TOPLINE China covered up the severity of *the virus* and delayed telling the World Health Organization (WHO) in order to import more medical supplies to respond to it, according to a new report by the Department for Homeland Security, seen by the Associated Press (AP).

China "intentionally concealed the severity" of the *virus*, while ramping up imports and decreasing exports of medical supplies according to the report, dated May 1, 2020, and seen by AP.

Chinese authorities also held off from telling the WHO that the unknown illness was a "contagion," to buy officials time to import more PPE [Personal Protective Equipment], including face masks and surgical gowns, the DHS report found.

The report adds that China denied "there were export restrictions" and delayed releasing its trade data, and that there was a "95% probability" that changes in China's trading behavior were not within normal range, AP reported.

The report comes after Secretary of State Mike Pompeo over the weekend doubled down on unsubstantiated claims from the Trump administration that the *virus* originated in a Wuhan lab. Last week, the director of national intelligence said there was no evidence that the *virus* was man made.

China's handling of the early stages of the pandemic - and its tight grip on the flow of information has been increasingly under the spotlight, with Germany, Australia and the EU calling for an investigation tracing the origins of the illness.

As the *pandemic* spread to the rest of the world, China resold the masks and other medical supplies it hoarded. These were sold at inflated prices to countries desperate for supplies. China is making billions of dollars from the pandemic further strengthening their position in world economies.

Americans were shocked that China has a strangle-hold on American supply chains for material and parts used in American manufacturing plants. As China shut down their factories to prevent the virus from spreading, it shut down our supply chains which forced plants in the U.S. to shut down.

Americans were outraged when they found out China might be unable to supply critical deliveries of prescription medicines to

U.S. pharmaceutical companies due to the impact of *the virus*. Hundreds of prescription drugs have been outsourced to China to save money. Another fear developed that China could use the threat of withholding deliveries of these drugs as a form of blackmail. As the potential for these threats became evident, several members of Congress began drafting legislative bills to bring American manufacturing and supply chain plants back to the U.S.

The following story is quoted from Fox News.

> **General Jack Keane: China 'Weaponized' Coronavirus to 'Destroy Western Democracies' Economies'**
>
> By Charles Creitz | Fox News May 29, 2020
>
> Fox News senior strategic analyst General Jack Keane told *"The Story"* Friday that Chinese President Xi Jinping had *"weaponized"* the spread of coronavirus around the world to destroy Western economies and stifle its competition.
>
> Keane explained to host Martha MacCallum that Xi, like many observers, was shocked by President Trump's defeat of Hillary Clinton in 2016 and a subsequent description of China as a strategic "competitor" to the U.S.
>
> According to Keane, Xi has spent the last four years "adjusting" to that new normal.
>
> "And I think the Trump Administration has been trying to get their sea-legs straight during this time frame, as well," he said. "But now, President XI sees clear-eyed what it is: that his ambitions are going to be stifled if he doesn't come out and really take a stand, and that is what he is doing here.

"It's in Hong Kong, which is the flash point in the front lines of this confrontation between the United States and China, to be sure. He has weaponized COVID-19."

"I mean, [Xi] actually used that disease to spread it around the world because he thought it would destroy Western democracies' economies, and he's been able to accomplish that," Keane went on.

"He wants the confrontation. He is looking for it because he knows full well he can't get to his strategic objectives unless he gets the United States and the Allies to back down, as they were doing in the past."

Keane noted that Xi came to power prior to Trump's presidency and at the time declared that he intends to fully dominate the Sino-Pacific region.

"For four years, there was no impediment to that, there were no obstacles, nobody was pushing back on it, despite the fact they were predatory in what they were doing, and the Trump administration came in."

China's has for many years had a long-term plan to further increase its world economic dominance. China has used unfair trade practices for the last twenty years to gain this dominance. However, China has minimal oil producing capability and is the world's largest importer of crude oil. To protect their economy, which is driven by fossil fuels, they have been increasing their presence in all Middle Eastern OPEC countries. China has loaned and invested billions of dollars in OPEC countries. These investments significantly increase China's influence over the economies in these countries.

To further ensure the stability of an oil trade route and greatly expand commerce, China started the *Belt and Road Initiative (BRI)* in 2013. BRI is sometimes referred to as the *New Silk*

Road project and it is one of the most ambitious infrastructure projects ever conceived with costs expected to be in the trillions of dollars. The vast collection of development and investment initiatives would build a trade route road which stretches from East Asia to Europe. The BRI will significantly expand China's economic and political influence.

Why is China important?

Revelation 9:17 describes an army of 200 million men marching on Jerusalem from the East. China has an army that size today. Before the Belt and Road Project, an army could not have marched through the rugged mountains between Israel and China. When the armies gather at Armageddon, China will have an economic interest in being there. This is another sign validating the Biblical accuracy of the ultimate Battle at Armageddon.

Let's start with a short explanation of God's love for humanity and His master plan for that great event – the Millennium.

Chapter 3

God's Love and Master Plan

God loves humanity and had a master plan in place to redeem us from sin and death before Adam and Eve sinned.

God has repeatedly demonstrated His relentless love and pursuit of humanity since creation. God sent His message of love to the people in unconditional and unchanging terms. Simply obey and serve Him, and He would bless and protect them.

God has been silent in His dealings with the Jewish people for approximately 2,000 years. The Jewish people and the nation of Israel are key components in God's master plan. God will demonstrate His love and faithfulness to ensure His promises are delivered to the unsaved remnant of Jewish people plus all of humanity.

As believers waiting for Jesus to return, we are admonished to maintain HOPE.

> "[13][keep] looking for the blessed hope and glorious appearing of our great God and Savior Jesus Christ." (Titus 2:13)

> "[18]The trials of this life will be over, and we will see that our present sufferings are not worth comparing with the glory that will be revealed in us." (Romans 8:18)

God created everything to display His glory for the delight of His human creations so they could declare His greatness. The book of Genesis records God's extraordinary display of sovereignty in speaking creation into being.

However, the Scriptures make it plain that God created a perfect world, but sin and evil desires came into the world as a result of the selfishness of man. God is a God of love, and He desired to create people to love and obey Him, but genuine love cannot exist unless individuals are given a free will with freedom of choice. Therefore, a choice has to be made to either accept or reject God's love.

This choice made the possibility of rejection a reality. When Adam and Eve disobeyed God, they brought sin into the world. Adam and Eve brought the evil effects of sin upon themselves by selfishly choosing to live their way instead of God's way.

Although sin abounds today, it is also temporary. Sin with its evil results will eventually be destroyed. Satan has attempted since the inception of Adam and Eve to put doubts in our hearts about God's love. Love is a uniquely human trait God created in us. Love can be overwhelmed by unforgiveness, bitterness, and hate. Satan cultivates these demonic characteristics through the deception of sin.

A new world is coming in which there will be no more tears or pain because all things will be made new. Believers will receive new bodies and all the effects of sin, aging, and disease will be eliminated. The paradise in the Garden of Eden that was lost will be restored. This is the eternal HOPE all believers should possess within their souls.

> "[3]*And I heard a loud voice from heaven saying, Behold, the tabernacle of God is with men, and He will dwell with them, and they shall be His people. God Himself will be*

> *with them and be their God. ⁴And God will wipe away every tear from their eyes; there shall be no more death, nor sorrow, nor crying. There shall be no more pain, for the former things have passed away. ⁵Then He who sat on the throne said, Behold, I make all things new." (Revelation 21:3-5)*

The Bible teaches us that Christ's resurrection body is the pattern for our resurrection body.

> *"²⁰For our citizenship is in heaven, from which also we eagerly wait for a Savior, the Lord Jesus Christ; ²¹who will transform the body of our humble state into conformity with the body of His glory." (Philippians 3:20-21)*

We know that Christ was raised in a physical body because the disciples ate with Him after the resurrection (Acts 10:41) and touched Him (Matthew 28:9). Also, Jesus declared that His resurrected body was physical and touchable.

> *"³⁹Behold My hands and My feet, that it is I Myself. Handle Me and see, for a spirit does not have flesh and bones as you see I have." (Luke 24:39)*

Since Christ's resurrection is the pattern of our resurrection, we will therefore be raised in a physical body in eternity as well.

Our bodies are not going to be thrown away. They are going to be renewed, restored, and revitalized. This is part of HOPE as believers.

> *"²³Not only that, but we also who have the first fruits of the Spirit, even we ourselves groan within ourselves, eagerly waiting for the adoption, the redemption of our body. ²⁴For we were saved in this hope, but hope that is seen is not hope; for why does one still hope for what he*

sees? *25But if we hope for what we do not see, we eagerly wait for it with perseverance." (Romans 8:23-25)*

Jesus speaks of the resurrection as involving the coming forth of individuals out of their tombs, which clearly indicates a physical concept of the resurrection.

"28Do not marvel at this; for the hour is coming in which all who are in the graves will hear His voice 29and come forth—those who have done good, to the resurrection of life, and those who have done evil, to the resurrection of condemnation." (John 5:28-29)

The Old Testament speaks of the resurrection as being physical.

"2And many of those who sleep in the dust of the earth shall awake, Some to everlasting life, Some to shame and everlasting contempt." (Daniel 12:2)

Job states it this way.

"25For I know that my Redeemer lives, And He shall stand at last on the earth; 26And after my skin is destroyed, this I know, That in my flesh I shall see God, 27Whom I shall see for myself, And my eyes shall behold, and not another." (Job 19:25-27)

Our lives on earth can be enhanced by looking forward to the resurrection and then residing in the Millennium and spending Eternity with God.

This chapter summarizes our HOPE as believers. It is going to be a glorious day when we meet Jesus. I am looking forward to it.

Are you?

Many of you are going to be alive when Jesus returns to get His bride, the Church. We will begin studying God's unfinished business pertaining to End Time prophecies, the Jewish people, the nation of Israel, and the unconditional promises which God made to Abraham and King David.

Now for a short overview of the Abrahamic Covenant, so its remaining promises can be revealed.

Chapter 4

God's Unfulfilled Promises

After Adam and Eve sinned, they were expelled from the Garden of Eden. One of their sons, Cain, killed his brother Abel and then lied to God about it. God punished Cain by condemning him to a life of wandering throughout the earth. Adam and Eve gave birth to another son, Seth.

Seth was a righteous man in God's sight and became known as a preacher of righteousness. Seth's descendants continued living righteous lives for many generations. Cain's descendants continued in his wicked ways. After multiple generations, intermarriage between the brother's descendants resulted in a generation of people filled with wickedness and sin.

Finally, God had enough of the wickedness and sin that was rampant on the earth, so He chose one man and his family to preserve humanity, Noah.

> "[5]Then Lord saw that the wickedness of man was great in the earth, and that every intent of the thoughts of his heart was only evil continually. [6]And the Lord was sorry that He had made man on the earth, and He was grieved in His heart." (Genesis 6:5-6)

Here are some sobering thoughts for you to consider about Noah's time and God's response to it. Wickedness was so bad that God chose to start the human race over. He instructed

Noah to build an ark to escape a coming flood. The ark enabled Noah, his family, and all the animals on the ark to survive the flood. God killed everyone else and every living creature in the flood.

The wrath of God will ultimately destroy non-believers and only by His *grace* do we receive *mercy* instead. God owes no one His mercy, which is why His *mercy* is called *grace*. Noah found favor in the eyes of the LORD *"because he was deemed to be righteous."* We also can receive mercy by believing in Jesus while living a righteous life.

The people of Noah's day had no idea God's judgment was about to come. Jesus said that in the last days, people will act in a similar manner (Matthew 24:37). Non-believers today are in the same situation facing God's pending wrath.

The descendants of Noah repopulated the Earth and they started building the Tower of Babel. Their desire was to reach to Heaven and be equal to God. They knew strength and protection was found in unity. God saw their evil intent and caused people to speak different languages. He then dispersed them to different parts of the world, so they could not complete the tower.

> *"[1]Now the whole earth had one language and one speech. [2]And it came to pass, as they journeyed from the east, that they found a plain in the land of Shinar, and they dwelt there. [3]Then they said to one another, Come, let us make bricks and bake them thoroughly. They had brick for stone, and they had asphalt for mortar. [4]And they said, Come, let us build ourselves a city, and a tower whose top is in the heavens; let us make a name for ourselves, lest we be scattered abroad over the face of the whole earth.*

> *⁵But the Lord came down to see the city and the tower which the sons of men had built. ⁶And the Lord said, Indeed the people are one and they all have one language, and this is what they begin to do; now nothing that they propose to do will be withheld from them. ⁷Come, let Us go down and there confuse their language, that they may not understand one another's speech.*
>
> *⁸So the Lord scattered them abroad from there over the face of all the earth, and they ceased building the city. ⁹Therefore its name is called Babel, because there the Lord confused the language of all the earth; and from there the Lord scattered them abroad over the face of all the earth." (Genesis 11:1-9)*

While it might appear that God's scattering of the peoples was a punishment, it was also a means of fulfilling His plan. From the beginning, God intended people to disperse across the world and populate it. Please remember this story because it has significance in the Millennium.

> *"²⁸Be fruitful and multiply, and fill the earth and subdue it." (Genesis 1:28).*

By scattering people after destroying the tower, this dispersion ultimately resulted in the different races and cultures of people we have today. If they had completed the tower, the result would have been:

> *"⁶...nothing that they propose to do will now be impossible for them." (Genesis 11:6)*

The sin the people would have been capable of conceiving is incomprehensible due to their wickedness and pride.

After the flood, God patiently pursued humanity seeking a relationship of righteousness, worship, and fellowship. However, instead of choosing to worship the living God, they chose to worship idols and follow the desires of their flesh. God continued this approach with humanity for approximately 340 years until He revealed Himself to Abraham.

Approximately 2,000 years had passed since the creation of Adam. God then called a man named Abram, who later was renamed Abraham, to carry out the next phase of God's master plan for humanity.

The Abrahamic Covenant

At the beginning of Genesis Chapter 12, God asked Abram to leave his home and country and He made Abram three promises: the promise of a relationship with Himself, numerous descendants, and land.

> *"[1]Now the Lord had said to Abram:*
> *Get out of your country,*
> *From your family*
> *And from your father's house,*
> *To a land that I will show you.*
> *[2]I will make you a great nation;*
> *I will bless you*
> *And make your name great;*
> *And you shall be a blessing.*
> *[3]I will bless those who bless you,*
> *And I will curse him who curses you;*
> *And in you all the families of the earth shall be blessed."*
> *(Genesis 12:1-3)*

These promises became known as the Abrahamic Covenant which contained unconditional blessings for all of Abraham's spiritual children. Abraham's posterity was to be made into a great nation, and all the families of the earth were to be blessed.

From Abraham, God created a new race, the Jews. Through this chosen race, God revealed more of His prophetic plan to bless humanity with a Savior, Jesus. Jesus was to come from the natural seed of Abraham's descendants and his grandson, Jacob. Ten of Jacob's sons and two of his grandsons became the twelve tribal leaders allotted land in the Promised Land we know today as Israel.

This was a major paradigm shift in God's master plan to offer salvation to humanity through the Jewish race.

There are also the spiritual seeds of Abraham who are not descendants of Jacob. Here is where the promise to bless *"all the families of the earth"* applies. This is clearly defined below.

> *"*[6]*...just as Abraham believed God, and it was accounted to him for righteousness. *[7]*Therefore know that only <u>those who are of faith are sons of Abraham</u>. *[8]*And the Scripture, foreseeing that <u>God would justify the Gentiles by faith</u>, preached the gospel to Abraham beforehand, saying, In you all the nations shall be blessed. *[9]*<u>So then those who are of faith are blessed with believing Abraham</u>."*
> *(Galatians 3:6-9)*

In other words, *"all the families of the earth"* are the *Jewish and Gentile* spiritual children of Abraham who believed in faith. Therefore, **all** will be blessed.

> *"*[28]*There is neither Jew nor Greek, there is neither slave nor free, there is neither male nor female; for you are all one in Christ Jesus. *[29]*<u>And if you are Christ's, then you are Abraham's seed, and heirs according to the promise</u>."*
> (Galatians 3:28)

The First Unfulfilled Promise

God promised Abraham land and it became known as the *Promised Land*. God defined the area the descendants of Abraham were to occupy.

> "*¹⁸On the same day the Lord made a covenant with Abram, saying: To your descendants I have given this land, from the river of Egypt to the great river, the River Euphrates - ¹⁹the Kenites, the Kenezzites, the Kadmonites, ²⁰the Hittites, the Perizzites, the Rephaim, ²¹the Amorites, the Canaanites, the Girgashites, and the Jebusites." (Genesis 15:18-21)*

The boundaries of the Promised Land extend from the Nile river in Egypt and Sudan to the Euphrates river which includes modern day Iraq.

This land was promised, but not given to Abram, but rather to his descendants. We know the promise was passed on to Isaac, then to Jacob (Israel) and his children (Genesis 28:10-15)

Abraham also had another son. God blessed Abraham's other son, Ishmael, with many children as well, and they became known as Ishmaelites. However, the Bible affirms that His covenant was passed through the Son of the Promise, Isaac.

> "*²Then the Lord appeared to him and said: Do not go down to Egypt; live in the land of which I shall tell you. ³Dwell in this land, and I will be with you and bless you; for to you and your descendants I give all these lands, and I will perform the oath which I swore to Abraham your father." (Genesis 26:2-3)*

Even though the boundaries of the land promised were clearly defined, Israel has never had control of *all of this land*. This is the first unfulfilled promise. They will not occupy *all the land* until after the Tribulation.

The promise of the land to be given *"to your descendants"* has no time limit. Therefore, the nation of Israel will acquire all of the land God promised sometime in the future.

The Second Unfulfilled Promise

Today, Israel is a powerful country in the Middle East. However, only by God's grace and mercy have the Arab nations not destroyed Israel. The rebirth of the nation of Israel in 1948 was the first significant sign of the beginning of the End Times.

The second End Time sign was prophesied by Jesus when He declared that *"wars and rumors of wars"* were to increase. War erupted immediately after the ratification of the U.N. resolution creating the new government of Israel. Arab armies from Lebanon, Syria, Iraq, and Egypt invaded Israel.

Every year since 1948, Israel and the Middle Eastern nations have been continuously in conflict. The nation of Israel has fought eight recognized wars, two Palestinian intifadas, and a series of armed conflicts.

While Israel is a small powerful country today, it is dependent on the United States for the procurement of key, high cost U.S. weapon systems, such as combat aircraft and missile defense systems. The U.S. supplies about thirty percent of the Israel's total defense budget. The nation of Israel today is not the nation God promised the Jewish people. In the Millennium and Eternity, Israel will become the most powerful country in the world.

The Third Unfulfilled Prophecy – The Tabernacle of David

God made the next unfulfilled prophecy to King David.

King David wanted to build a permanent house of worship for the Lord. God saw David's heart, so He sent Nathan, the prophet, with a message to David. God told David that he was not to build the place of worship, but a future son would build the temple.

"[12]When your days are fulfilled and you rest with your fathers, I will set up your seed after you, who will come from your body, and I will establish his kingdom. [13]He shall build a house for My name, and I will establish the throne of his kingdom forever. [14]I will be his Father, and he shall be My son. If he commits iniquity, I will chasten him with the rod of men and with the blows of the sons of men. [15]But My mercy shall not depart from him, as I took it from Saul, whom I removed from before you.

[16]And your house and your kingdom shall be established forever before you. Your throne shall be established forever." (II Samuel 7:12-16)

"[15]And with this the words of the prophets agree, just as it is written:

[16]After this I will return and will rebuild the tabernacle of David, which has fallen down;

I will rebuild its ruins, And I will set it up; [17]So that the rest of mankind may seek the Lord.

Even all the Gentiles who are called by My name, Says the Lord who does all these things." (Acts 15:13-17)

Jesus will sit upon the Throne of David after the Battle of Armageddon at end of the Tribulation. Therefore, the Tabernacle will be rebuilt at the start of the Millennium.

The next chapter will explain why God has unfinished business with the non-believing Jews and the nation of Israel.

Chapter 5

The Mosaic Covenant and God Turns His Back on Israel

Jacob, Abraham's grandson had twelve sons and Joseph was his favorite. Joseph's ten older brothers hated him. They plotted to kill him, but instead sold him as a slave. Joseph ended up in Egypt. God gave Joseph favor in everything he did. God elevated Joseph so he became a powerful ruler in Egypt, second only to Pharaoh.

In about 1,700 B. C., a severe famine threatened the existence of Jacob's family. He sent ten of his sons into Egypt to buy grain. They appeared before Joseph to complete their purchase. They did not recognize Joseph, but Joseph recognized them. He did not reveal his identity to them.

Joseph inquired about their family. They told Joseph about their father and the younger brother they left at home. Joseph inflicted a degree of revenge on his brothers by accusing them of being spies and threating to put them in prison. He declared Simeon was to remain in prison until they brought their younger brother to Egypt. He then sent them home with their grain, but secretly placed their payments into their saddlebags. When Joseph's brothers discovered the money, their fear of Joseph increased greatly.

The famine intensified in Israel, so the brothers returned with their younger brother, Benjamin. Finally Joseph revealed himself as their brother. Joseph then arranged for His Father and all his family to move to Egypt. In the years following, the Jews multiplied greatly and prospered.

After Joseph died, Pharaohs came to power who did not know the story of how Joseph saved Egypt from the famine. They began to fear the Jews, and forced them into slavery.

God heard the Jews appeals for deliverance from the oppression of slavery, so He sent Moses to lead them back to the *Promised Land* of Israel after 400 years.

As they traveled back to Israel from Egypt, God gave Moses the Ten Commandments. Then God made a covenant with Moses and the Jewish people. God promised blessing for obedience, and curses for disobedience. The blessings and curses are explained in detail in Deuteronomy 28. The covenant became known as the Mosaic Covenant.

God presented to Moses a plan for systematic temple sacrifices and worship rituals administered by Levite priests. The Ten Commandments were expanded into *The Law*. *The Law* regulated the priesthood, sacrifices, rituals, and offerings. Provisions were made to administer social judgments and religious ordinances based upon the Law.

Additional civil and ceremonial laws were developed from the Mishnah and Talmud to be used by civil leaders to govern the people.

The Levitical Feasts

In Leviticus 3, God spoke to Moses to establish the *"feasts of the Lord."* The feasts were designed to be ceremonies symbolizing the coming Messiah. The Messiah would bring the blessings to all the nations God promised to Abraham.

The feasts established were Passover, Unleavened Bread, First Fruits, Feast of Weeks (Pentecost), Feast of Trumpets (Rosh Hashanah), Day of Atonement (Yom Kippur), and the Feast of Tabernacles (Booths). These feasts are an essential element in our final 2,000 years. Each feast is described in a later chapter.

The Mosaic covenant was a conditional covenant, meaning that both parties were responsible to fulfill a duty to the other. The people were responsible to follow the Law. In return, God promised to abundantly bless and protect Israel (Exodus 19:5-8).

The conditional nature of the Mosaic covenant made it very different from the Abrahamic Covenant, which was unconditional. In an unconditional covenant, God's favor, provisions, and blessings are based on His promises rather than on the actions of the people.

The Mosaic Covenant was a covenant of works with impossible requirements to meet. Therefore, it was a ministry of *"condemnation and death" and it* ended with the death of Jesus.

> *"[7]But if the ministry of death, written and engraved on stones, was glorious, so that the children of Israel could not look steadily at the face of Moses because of the glory of his countenance, which glory was passing away, [8]how will the ministry of the Spirit not be more glorious? [9]For if the ministry of condemnation had glory, the ministry of righteousness exceeds much more in glory." (2 Corinthians 3:7-9)*

The Law was a dramatic change for Jews. They now had rules, regulations, and rituals for every aspect of their lives. They had prescribed ordinances and worship practices to follow they previously did not have.

The descendants of Abraham continually reverted to idol worship and sin.

God demonstrated His grace and mercy continually during this period. God sent multiple prophets to forewarn the people to repent of their sinful ways and turn back to God. His messages of love to the people were unconditional and unchanging. Simply obey and serve Him, and He would bless and protect them.

They failed to observe the Law, so God sent His Son Jesus to offer salvation to all people.

God turns his back on the Jews.

Jesus came to the world as the promised Messiah, but the Jews rejected Him. They crucified Him. When the Jews rejected Jesus as their Messiah, it cut off non-believing Jews from the blessing of the Abrahamic Covenant. After the death of His Son, God turned His back on the Jews. God then directed His attention to the Gentiles for the next 2,000 years.

Daniel prophesied the crucifixion, the destruction of Jerusalem and the nation of Israel that followed after Jesus' death. He described how Jesus was going to be rejected with the term, "*cut off*", which had special meaning to the Jews.

> "*26Then after the sixty-two weeks the Messiah will be <u>cut off</u> and have nothing, and the people of the prince who is to come will destroy the city and the sanctuary. And its end will come with a flood; even to the end there will be war; desolations are determined." (Daniel 9:26)*

Jewish commentaries state the term "cut off" is used for carrying out the death penalty on a king or the high priest. It also applies to a criminal. The prophecy clearly points to the crucifixion of Jesus. At His crucifixion Jesus *had nothing* in the sense that Israel had rejected Him, therefore His kingdom could not be instituted at that time.

The Mosaic Covenant did not terminate the Abrahamic Covenant.

God's master plan has provisions to fulfill every unconditional promise, and to offer the Jews one final chance to accept Jesus as their promised Messiah.

The crucifixion of Jesus renders the Old Covenant (Mosaic) void, but He makes provision for a replacement covenant.

The New Covenant

Jesus' declaration of the New Covenant terminated the Old Covenant. The Old Covenant served its purpose, and has been replaced by a better covenant.

> "[22]*by so much more Jesus has become a surety of a better covenant." (Hebrews 7:22)*

> "[15]*And for this reason He is the Mediator of the new covenant, by means of death, for the redemption of the transgressions under the first covenant, that those who are called may receive the promise of the eternal inheritance." (Hebrews 9:15)*

Entering into the New Covenant requires believing that Jesus is the Son of God and He died for you. Forgiveness of sins comes only comes through confession of sin with repentance. Then, the blood of Jesus cleanses and washes away all sin. The new believer receives an eternal inheritance to live with God forever starting in the Millennium and continuing throughout Eternity.

The New Covenant provides believers direct access to God through Jesus.

> "[20]Likewise He also took the cup after supper, saying, This cup is the new covenant in My blood, which is shed for you." (Luke 22:20)

The *times of the Gentiles* started with Jesus' death. God showed His grief by tearing the Temple veil in half from top to bottom. This act was a well-known symbol for grieving over the death of a loved one. The interpretation of God splitting the veil was a sign to the Jews that the Temple system was now defunct and obsolete. As prophesied, Jerusalem and the Temple were destroyed about forty years later. Israel ceased to exist as a nation.

Jesus started building His Church when His ministry started. After His death, thousands of Gentiles came to be believers. The early Jewish converts combined with the Gentile believers became the foundation of the early first century Church.

God imbedded in the Old Testament for the Jews multiple scriptures pointing to the *end of this age* and descriptions of *the age to come*. God gave us a specific timeline from the death of Jesus until the end of current age or *this age.*

We are within a few short years of being at the end of *this age*.

We will begin by studying the prophecies of Daniel that define when the age ends.

Chapter 6

Daniel's 70 Weeks Contain the Timeline for End Time Events

Now we are going to examine one of the most important prophecies about the end of our current age. When completed, it brings us to the start of the Millennium. Daniel had lived for nearly 70 years in Babylon and as old man was aware of this prophecy in Jeremiah:

> "*10For thus says the Lord: After seventy years are completed at Babylon, I will visit you and perform My good word toward you, and cause you to return to this place." (Jeremiah 29:10)*

Israel was approaching seventy years in exile. While praying a powerful prayer of repentance for the people of Israel and seeking God for deliverance from their years in Babylon, Daniel received from the angel Gabriel this famous prophecy.

> "*24Seventy weeks are determined for your people and for your holy city, To finish the transgression, To make an end of sins, To make reconciliation for iniquity, To bring in everlasting righteousness, To seal up vision and prophecy, And to anoint the Most Holy.*
>
> *25Know therefore and understand, That from the going forth of the command To restore and build Jerusalem Until Messiah the Prince, There shall be <u>seven weeks</u>*

and sixty-two weeks; The street shall be built again, and the wall, Even in troublesome times.

²⁶And after the sixty-two weeks Messiah shall be cut off, but not for Himself; And the people of the prince who is to come shall destroy the city and the sanctuary. The end of it shall be with a flood, and till the end of the war desolations are determined.

²⁷Then he shall confirm a covenant with many for one week; But in the middle of the week He shall bring an end to sacrifice and offering. And on the wing of abominations shall be one who makes desolate, Even until the consummation, which is determined, Is poured out on the desolate." (Daniel 9:24-27)

An understanding of the timeline of the 70 weeks enables a greater understanding of all End Time prophecies contained in numerous books of the Bible.

The Hebrew word for week is *shabua* which can mean a week of seven days or, it can mean years depending upon the context in which it is used. A graphic example can be seen in Genesis 29:27 where one week is seven years. This passage is about the story of Jacob working for Laban in order to gain his daughter Rachel as his wife. He worked seven years to get Rachel, but was tricked into marrying Leah, Rachel's older sister. Then he had to work seven more years to get Rachel. Finally, he worked seven more years to get his flock started. Each seven year segment in Hebrew means one week.

"²⁷Fulfill her week, and we will give you this one also for the service which you will serve with me still another seven years." (Genesis 29:27)

Each one of Daniel's 70 weeks in Hebrew should be interpreted as a 7 year segment of time. Therefore, *70 weeks* is calculated as 70 x 7 years equals 490 years.

Verse 25 breaks the 490 years down into two periods of 7 and 62 weeks. Let's do the math for the years for each period:

	Weeks	7 Years Per Week	Years
	7	7	49
	62	7	434
Totals	69	7	483

The 483 years is the period of time needed to restore and rebuild Jerusalem before Messiah, the Prince of Peace, comes. This is referring to Jesus making His entrance into Jerusalem on Palm Sunday before His crucifixion.

However, there remains one week which is described in verse 27.

> "*[27]Then he shall confirm a covenant with many for one week; But in the middle of the week He shall bring an end to sacrifice and offering. And on the wing of abominations shall be one who makes desolate, Even until the consummation, which is determined, Is poured out on the desolate.*"

This week is the seven years of Tribulation. Revelation 11:2 refers to the three and one half years as forty two months and then in verse 3, it is called 1,260 days. In Revelation 12:6 it is 1,260 days and then in verse 14, time and times and half a time.

Daniel 7:25 first used the phrase time and times and half a time. A time equals one year, times equals two years, and half a time equals one half year. Adding these together you get three and one half years (1 time + 2 times + ½ time = 3 ½ years).

Confusing?

It can be!

To make it easy to understand, just remember anywhere you see one of these time references, associate it with three and one half years.

The *"covenant"* in verse 27 is the seven year peace agreement or covenant Israel enters into with the Antichrist. In verse 26, the prince is the Antichrist who destroys the Temple when he breaks the peace agreement in the middle of the week. The Antichrist does this after three and one half years, which is the middle of the seven years. He stops sacrifices and becomes an abomination to God and the Jews by taking control of the Temple and declaring himself to be God. Then the Antichrist begins intense persecution of the Jews for the remainder of the Tribulation.

If you continue reading through the rest of the verse, you come to the reason for the 490 year total is to *"to bring in everlasting righteousness."* This prophecy pertains to the Millennium and Eternity.

Gabriel delivers the prophecy of 70 weeks to Daniel in approximately 539 B.C. The Jews were now captives of the Persians. Daniel's prayer was answered when King Cyrus of Persia signed a decree allowing the Jews to return to Jerusalem in 538 B.C. and rebuild their Temple. However, when they arrived in Jerusalem, it was in ruins. When they started rebuilding the wall and the city, some of the non-Jewish people in the area protested and sent appeals against the rebuilding to Persia. This stopped the rebuilding of the city and wall.

In 444 B.C. after approximately 95 years, Nehemiah described to King Artaxerxes how Judah in Palestine had been partly repopulated by Jews. These are the descendants of the original Jews released from their exile in Babylon. The Temple at Jerusalem had been rebuilt, but the Jewish community there was dispirited and defenseless against its non-Jewish neighbors because the Jerusalem walls had not been rebuilt.

> *"5And I said to the king, If it pleases the king, and if your servant has found favor in your sight, I ask that you send me to Judah, to the city of my fathers' tombs, that I may rebuild it." (Nehemiah 2:5)*

The king responded with the command to rebuild Jerusalem, which was believed to be formalized in 445 B.C.

Sir Robert Anderson in 1894 published *The Coming Prince* which unlocked the key to the calculation of the 70 weeks. In the book, he revealed how he discovered one Bible month equals 30 days, so one year is 360 days. Our solar based calendar year equates to 365.25 days. Using a lunar calendar with 360 days in a year, Jesus entered into Jerusalem on Nisan 10, 32 A.D. The people hailed Him as the coming King, but the Jewish leaders tried to *cut Him off* from entering Jerusalem with such acclaim (Luke 19:28-44). The detailed calculation for the 483 years is depicted in Book 3, *The Date of the Rapture*.

With this adjustment, the prophecy of Jesus making His entrance to Jerusalem on Palm Sunday was accurate within four days on the current Hebrew calendar. If you use NASA data to pinpoint new moon dates to improve the accuracy of the Jewish calendar, the difference is one day.

The crucifixion of Jesus ended the 69th week of Daniel's timeline. God then ceased dealing with Israel as a nation. The Jews were *cut off* from God because of their unbelief for the next 2,000 years. Jerusalem and the Temple were destroyed, and the nation of Israel ceased to exist. This happened thirty eight years later as predicted by both Daniel and Jesus.

> "[26] And after the sixty-two weeks Messiah shall be cut off, but not for Himself; And the people of the prince who is to come shall destroy the city and the sanctuary. The end of it shall be with a flood, And till the end of the war desolations are determined." (Daniel 9:26)

> "[43] Therefore I tell you, the kingdom of God will be taken away from you and given to [another] people who will produce the fruit of it." (Matthew 21:43 KJV)

> "[37] O Jerusalem, Jerusalem, the one who kills the prophets and stones those who are sent to her! How often I wanted to gather your children together, as a hen gathers her chicks under her wings, but you were not willing! [38] See! Your house is left to you desolate; [39] for I say to you, you shall see Me no more till you say, Blessed is He who comes in the name of the Lord!" (Matthew 23:37-39)

Between the time of the Rapture and the Second Coming of Jesus to the earth, Daniel's 70th Week of seven years will end this age. The Second Coming of Jesus to the earth comes at the end of the week, and it cannot take place until all these Tribulation scriptures are fulfilled.

These prophecies were fulfilled exactly as predicted. However, the Jews are still *cut off* from God. They don't have their Temple, and they refuse to acknowledge Jesus as their Messiah.

Next, we will begin the discussion of the prophecies that deal with non-believers and the restoration of the Jews and the nation of Israel.

Chapter 7

Daniel, Matthew, and Revelation Part 1 The Dream

King Nebuchadnezzar's Dream

The relationships of prophecies within the books of Daniel, Matthew, and Revelation can be very confusing. Many people get frustrated and stop trying to understand the prophetic portions of these books. There is an amazing connection between them. God not only clarifies, but emphasizes the importance of the End Time events. He goes into great detail to explain how they fit into His plan for the redemption of humanity.

God has a defined timeline for the pending judgments in the Tribulation, and He will reveal it to those who seek to understand it. God deemed it important by repeating the warnings using different prophets. The Tribulation is going to be a terrible bloodbath, and God wants everyone to avoid it by believing and trusting in Him.

You will be shown a comparison of these prophecies made by Daniel, Jesus, and the Apostle John to show how they depict the same evolving story of God's master plan of redemption. **Whenever God wants to make an important point, He reinforces by it restating it.**

We will start by examining the prophecies given to Daniel by God when he interpreted a dream for King Nebuchadnezzar.

Daniel was a young man approximately seventeen years old when he was sent into exile in Babylon with the remnants of the nation of Israel in approximately 604 B.C. God gave Daniel tremendous wisdom and knowledge. The Babylonians recognized that he was a wise young man, so they trained him in their ways. Later in life, they placed him in the council of wise men. Daniel ascended to a position of prominence and power as the Chief of the Wise Men and served four different kings in Babylon.

In Daniel Chapter 2, King Nebuchadnezzar had a dream, but he couldn't remember it.

> "*³And the king said to them, I have had a dream, and my spirit is anxious to know the dream. ⁴Then the Chaldeans spoke to the king in Aramaic, O king, live forever! Tell your servants the dream, and we will give the interpretation.*
>
> *⁵The king answered and said to the Chaldeans, My decision is firm: if you do not make known the dream to me, and its interpretation, you shall be cut in pieces, and your houses shall be made an ash heap. ⁶However, if you tell the dream and its interpretation, you shall receive from me gifts, rewards, and great honor. Therefore tell me the dream and its interpretation." (Daniel 2:3-6)*

None of his wise men could reveal the dream to him. The King became furious and was going to kill all the wise men, including Daniel. Daniel prayed and God revealed the dream to him which contained four kingdoms.

If you will, in your mind go back in time and put yourself in Daniel's position standing before the King. You are about to deliver a very complicated dream to a King who could not remember it. He also had the power to immediately have you executed if he didn't agree with your explanation of the dream. Even if you got it correct, and he didn't like either the dream or what you said, he could still have you killed. What would your heart rate be and would you put your life on the line like Daniel did? I love this story because it encourages me to have faith and trust God's word in difficult situations.

Daniel – The Four Kingdoms

Here is the dream Daniel revealed to King Nebuchadnezzar.

> "[31] You, O king, were watching; and behold, a great image! This great image, whose splendor was excellent, stood before you; and its form was awesome. [32] This image's head was of fine gold, its chest and arms of silver, its belly and thighs of bronze, [33] its legs of iron, its feet partly of iron and partly of clay. [34] You watched while a stone was cut out without hands, which struck the image on its feet of iron and clay, and broke them in pieces. [35] Then the iron, the clay, the bronze, the silver, and the gold were crushed together, and became like chaff from the summer threshing floors; the wind carried them away so that no trace of them was found. And the stone that struck the image became a great mountain and filled the whole earth." (Daniel 2:31-35)

Next, Daniel tells the King the interpretation of the dream.

Daniel told Nebuchadnezzar the head of gold was his kingdom, and after his kingdom, three more would come. We now know from studying history the kingdoms following after Nebuchadnezzar's were the Medo-Persian, Greek and Roman. Each of these kingdoms ruled much of the world during their existence. The Roman kingdom was notorious for the brutality it used to crush the nations it conquered. The Romans had little sympathy for the people of the conquered nations. They sent millions of men, women and children into slavery. As one commentator, John F. Walvoord, put it, *"The glory of Rome was built on the misery of its conquered peoples."*

The stone in Daniel 2:35 that struck the image and became a great mountain is significant to our study. The stone represents the future eternal kingdom God will establish.

The four kingdoms in the dream have come and gone, so what kingdom has to be conquered before God sets up His eternal kingdom?

Daniel gives part of the answer in Daniel Chapter 2 and expands on it in Chapter 7 in a vision God gave him. It is a new fifth kingdom.

> *"[41]Whereas you saw the feet and toes, partly of potter's clay and partly of iron, the kingdom shall be divided; yet the strength of the iron shall be in it, just as you saw the iron mixed with ceramic clay. [42]And as the toes of the feet were partly of iron and partly of clay, so the kingdom shall be partly strong and partly fragile. [43]As you saw iron mixed with ceramic clay, they will mingle with the seed of men; but they will not adhere to one another, just as iron does not mix with clay. [44]<u>And in the days of these kings the God of heaven will set up a kingdom which shall never be destroyed; and the kingdom shall not be left to other people; it shall break in pieces and consume all these kingdoms, and it shall stand forever</u>." (Daniel 2:41-44)*

Please note that there is a subtle difference in the explanation of the dream Daniel gave to Nebuchadnezzar versus the interpretation. In describing the dream, the toes and feet were not succinctly described to the King, but they were described in detail in the interpretation. Plus, the toes are fully explained in Chapter 7. They obviously contain a powerful message.

Daniel is describing a fifth and future kingdom which is clear in Daniel 2:44 and it is not the Kingdom of God. It will exist <u>*in the days of these kings,*</u> and then God <u>*shall break in pieces and consume all these kingdoms and it shall stand forever*</u>. These kings are the ten nations comprising a future kingdom. God then breaks or destroys these kingdoms.

The phrase *"in the days of these kings"* and the ten toes of iron and clay refer to a future form of the revived Roman Empire. This new coalition will show both strength and weakness. The ten toes refer to ten kings or nations that will rule over the revived Roman kingdom. The European Union (E.U.) will probably evolve to be the governing body or kingdom to fulfill this portion of the prophecy. The framework of the E.U. is already in place, so it will be easy for the Antichrist to take it over.

The first mention of the eternal kingdom in Daniel occurs in verse 44. This verse refers to the 1,000 year Millennial Reign of Jesus.

Matthew / Revelation – The Four Kingdoms

Jesus and John were alive during the Roman kingdom, or the fourth kingdom, and spoke frequently about Roman rule. Neither make specific references to the first three kingdoms in Daniel's dream. They were past history and so they had no reason to discuss them.

Jesus made multiple references to Daniel 7. Jesus predicted the future destruction of the Temple (Matthew 24:2), He tells the Jews to flee when they see the *abomination of desolation* (Matthew 24:15), and they *will see the Son of Man coming on the clouds* (Matthew 24:30).

Daniel's Vision of the Four Beasts

Many years later Daniel had a vision like Nebuchadnezzar's dream of the four beasts.

Now, we will examine the four beasts and their significance to End Time events.

> "³And four great beasts came up from the sea, each different from the other. ⁴The first was like a lion, and had eagle's wings. I watched till its wings were plucked off; and it was lifted up from the earth and made to stand on two feet like a man, and a man's heart was given to it.
>
> ⁵And suddenly another beast, a second, like a bear. It was raised up on one side, and had three ribs in its mouth between its teeth. And they said thus to it: Arise, devour much flesh!
>
> ⁶After this I looked, and there was another, like a leopard, which had on its back four wings of a bird. The beast also had four heads, and dominion was given to it.
>
> ⁷After this I saw in the night visions, and behold, a fourth beast, dreadful and terrible, exceedingly strong. It had huge iron teeth; it was devouring, breaking in pieces, and trampling the residue with its feet. It was different from all the beasts that were before it, and it had ten horns. ⁸I was considering the horns, and there was another horn, <u>a little one, coming up among them</u>, before whom three of the first horns were plucked out by the roots. And there, in this horn, were eyes like the eyes of a man, and <u>a mouth speaking pompous words</u>." (Daniel 7:3-8)

The first beast was representative of King Nebuchadnezzar of Babylon. Its rise to a human like status reflects Nebuchadnezzar's recovery from the seven years God sent him to live like a beast in isolation. He ate grass like an ox and was probably insane during this time. God did this because of Nebuchadnezzar's pride over his might and power. God restored his sanity and kingdom after he found the true nature of God (Daniel 4:34–35).

The next beast was a bear that devours flesh, which symbolized how nations were conquered by the Medo-Persian Empire. The raised up of side of the creature indicated that one of the kingdom's parts (Persia) dominated. The three ribs in the creature's mouth represented the devoured nations of Babylon, Lydia, and Egypt.

The third beast was *like a leopard*, except it has four bird-like wings on its back and four heads. It represented Greece, which swiftly conquered the nations. The four heads symbolized the four-way division of the empire following Alexander the Great's death.

The fourth beast will occur in the future and represents the revived Roman empire.

> "²³And in the latter time of their kingdom, When the transgressors have reached their fullness, A king shall arise, Having fierce features, Who understands sinister schemes. ²⁴His power shall be mighty, but not by his own power; He shall destroy fearfully, and shall prosper and thrive; He shall destroy the mighty, and also the holy people. ²⁵Through his cunning He shall cause deceit to prosper under his rule; And he shall exalt himself in his heart. He shall destroy many in their prosperity. <u>He shall even rise against the Prince of princes; But he shall be broken without human means.</u>" (Daniel 8:23-25)

The ten horns represent the nations in the revived Roman Empire, which will be resurrected before the Tribulation begins. The little horn represents a future time when the Antichrist establishes and controls a one-world religious system through the false prophet.

> "*^{19}Then I wished to know the truth about the fourth beast which was different from all the others, exceedingly dreadful, with its teeth of iron and its nails of bronze, which devoured, broke in pieces, and trampled the residue with its feet; ^{20}and the ten horns that were on its head, and <u>the other horn</u> which came up, before which three fell, namely, that horn which had eyes and a mouth <u>which spoke pompous words,</u> whose appearance was greater than his fellows.*
>
> *^{21}I was watching; and the same horn was making war against the saints, and prevailing against them,"* (Daniel 7:19-21)

Matthew - The Four Beasts

Please note: Daniel describes four beasts, but John only describes two beasts in Revelation. Matthew does not use the imagery of either Daniel or John in describing the four beasts, but Matthew quoted Jesus to describe the impact the beasts will make.

Matthew describes the Antichrist, which is the fourth beast in Daniel. The following are Jesus' words:

> "*^{15}Therefore when you see the abomination of desolation, spoken of by Daniel the prophet, standing in the holy place (whoever reads, let him understand)."* (Matthew 24:15)

Jesus describes the false prophet, the beast of the sea in Revelation 13:1-4 perfectly.

"24For false christs and false prophets will rise and show great signs and wonders to deceive, if possible, even the elect." (Matthew 24:24)

Revelation – The Four Beasts of Daniel and the Two Beasts in Revelation

The Apostle John describes two beasts, one coming out of the land (earth) and the other out of the sea. The first beast described by John is the same as the fourth beast in Daniel which is the revived Roman Empire. John's second beast, the false prophet, was not described by Daniel.

The first beast in Revelation is the Antichrist coming out the depths of hell.

"7When they finish their testimony, the beast that ascends out of the bottomless pit will make war against them, overcome them, and kill them." (Revelation 11:7)

"11Then I saw another beast coming up out of the earth, and he had two horns like a lamb and spoke like a dragon. 12And he exercises all the authority of the first beast in his presence, and causes the earth and those who dwell in it to worship the first beast, whose deadly wound was healed. 13He performs great signs, so that he even makes fire come down from heaven on the earth in the sight of men. 14And he deceives those who dwell on the earth by those signs which he was granted to do in the sight of the beast, telling those who dwell on the earth to make an image to the beast who was wounded by the sword and lived. 15He was granted power to give breath to the image of the beast, that the image of the beast should both speak and cause as many as would not worship the image of the beast to be killed. 16He causes all, both small and great, rich and poor, free and slave, to

receive a mark on their right hand or on their foreheads, [17]and that no one may buy or sell except one who has the mark or the name of the beast, or the number of his name." (Daniel 13:11-17)

In Revelation, the term *beast* can describe two similar entities. Sometimes *the beast* refers to an empire. Later references to *the beast* in Revelation picture an individual in disguise as a man, but can be either the Antichrist or false prophet. The Antichrist becomes a political leader and head of the beastly empire.

In Daniel's vision, the Antichrist is the *little horn* that rises from the head of the terrifying beast (Daniel 7:8). However, the beast's time is short. According to Revelation 13:5 and Daniel 7:25, he only has absolute authority for three and a half years.

The second beast coming out of the sea is the false prophet.

"[1]Then I stood on the sand of the sea. And I saw a beast rising up out of the sea, having seven heads and ten horns, and on his horns ten crowns, and on his heads a blasphemous name. [2]Now the beast which I saw was like a leopard, his feet were like the feet of a bear, and his mouth like the mouth of a lion. The dragon gave him his power, his throne, and great authority. [3]And I saw one of his heads as if it had been mortally wounded, and his deadly wound was healed. And all the world marveled and followed the beast. [4]So they worshiped the dragon who gave authority to the beast; and they worshiped the beast, saying, Who is like the beast? Who is able to make war with him?" (Revelation 13:1-4)

The false prophet will be the third party in Satan's unholy trinity. This unholy trinity will be Satan, the Antichrist, and the False Prophet.

Satan is arranging his Great Tribulation kingdom to mock God's Holy Trinity of the Father, Son, and Holy Spirit. Satan will take the role of God the Father, the Antichrist will take the role of Jesus, and the False Prophet will take the role of the Holy Spirit.

The false prophet's mission is to exalt the Antichrist so people will worship him. Thus, the false prophet assumes a role like the Holy Spirit's role to draw people to Jesus. The false prophet will be the one to lead the world to serve the Antichrist.

At the middle of the Tribulation, when the *abomination of desolation* occurs, Satan demands people worship him. Satan has always wanted to be like God. This is his one and only chance to actually play God in the last forty-two months on earth. Satan probably stops merely controlling the Antichrist and physically manifests himself within the mind and body of the Antichrist.

An angel carrying the seven bowl judgments spoke to John these words which further describe John's fourth beast:

> "[3]*...And I saw a woman sitting on a scarlet beast which was full of names of blasphemy, having seven heads and ten horns. [4]The woman was arrayed in purple and scarlet, and adorned with gold and precious stones and pearls, having in her hand a golden cup full of abominations and the filthiness of her fornication. [5]And on her forehead a name was written:*
>
> *MYSTERY, BABYLON THE GREAT,*
> *THE MOTHER OF HARLOTS*
> *AND OF THE ABOMINATIONS*
> *OF THE EARTH.*
>
> *[6]I saw the woman, drunk with the blood of the saints and with the blood of the martyrs of Jesus. And when I saw her, I marveled with great amazement.*

⁷But the angel said to me, Why did you marvel? I will tell you the mystery of the woman and of the beast that carries her, which has the seven heads and the ten horns. ⁸The beast that you saw was, and is not, and will ascend out of the bottomless pit and go to perdition. And those who dwell on the earth will marvel, whose names are not written in the Book of Life from the foundation of the world, when they see the beast that was, and is not, and yet is.

⁹Here is the mind which has wisdom: The seven heads are seven mountains on which the woman sits. ¹⁰There are also seven kings. Five have fallen, one is, and the other has not yet come. And when he comes, he must continue a short time. ¹¹The beast that was, and is not, is himself also the eighth, and is of the seven, and is going to perdition.

¹²The ten horns which you saw are ten kings who have received no kingdom as yet, but they receive authority for one hour as kings with the beast. ¹³These are of one mind, and they will give their power and authority to the beast. ¹⁴These will make war with the Lamb, and the Lamb will overcome them, for He is Lord of lords and King of kings; and those who are with Him are called, chosen, and faithful.

¹⁵Then he said to me, The waters which you saw, where the harlot sits, are peoples, multitudes, nations, and tongues. ¹⁶And the ten horns which you saw on the beast, these will hate the harlot, make her desolate and naked, eat her flesh and burn her with fire. ¹⁷For God has put it into their hearts to fulfill His purpose, to be of one mind, and to give their kingdom to the beast, until the words of God are fulfilled." (Revelation 17:7-17)

The ten horns or ten kings, unite to form a powerful union possibly by taking over the European Union. The beast, most likely the Antichrist, eventually becomes head of this Union, the revived Roman Empire. They all hate religious Babylon (represented as the harlot), and destroy her. Her destruction is planned because the Antichrist desires to establish his own one-world religion. The Antichrist has plans to initiate a demand to the world that everyone must worship him (Revelation 13:11–12). Therefore, he views religious Babylon as competition.

The seven heads of the beast are described as seven mountains, which is where the harlot sits. This could refer to the seven mountains that surround Rome, serving as the center of her false religious system.

The revived Roman Empire is described by John as a *scarlet beast* that carries the harlot dressed in scarlet. The scarlet beast is commonly referred to as the *Whore of Babylon*. Scarlet is associated with immorality and sin, particularly prostitution or adultery. The harlot is a symbol for the false religion that originates in Rome, but has spread throughout the world. The harlot also represents the unspiritual, ungodly religious character of the world at the beginning of the Tribulation.

The harlot has committed adultery with the *"kings of the earth."* The harlot's false religion has been embraced by the world's rulers and influential people. The reference to being drunk with the wine may refer to those kings or people in authority who are drunk with the power they receive from worshiping the false god of the false religion.

The inference to *"drunk with the blood of the saints"* implies people on the earth experience her wrath. Those who oppose the worldwide religion are killed.

The Antichrist is a political figure. It appears that an assassination attempt is made on his life and he incurs an apparent fatal wound. The Antichrist gains the world's attention by his miraculous recovery from the wound (Revelation 13:3, 12, 14). The Antichrist uses this notoriety to overthrow the harlot because of his desire for the world to worship him instead of God.

The Antichrist with his ten nations destroy the false religious systems. This leaves the harlot, the religious Babylon, desolate and naked. When they kill off her religious system, they confiscate all her wealth and kill the harlot.

The Antichrist then declares he is God, assumes the role of God, and demands everyone worship him. Jesus tells us, *"his deception will be so great that even the elect will fall for it."* (Matthew 24:24).

Those who refuse to worship the Antichrist by not accepting his mark of 666 will be unable to buy and sell, thereby making their survival very difficult (Revelation 13:16–17).

The fourth beast of Daniel 7 also had ten horns which represents the ten nations of the revived Roman empire. These references strengthen the identity of this beast, the Antichrist, in Revelation.

The Four Living Creatures of Revelation Compared to Daniel's Four Beasts

Revelation describes four living creatures some people mistakenly refer to as beasts. Rather than describe these creatures in the Revelation chapter, the distinction needs to be made here. Many people think of these heavenly beings as beasts like the four in Daniel, which results in confusion.

> "*⁵And from the throne proceeded lightnings, thunderings, and voices. Seven lamps of fire were burning before the throne, which are the seven Spirits of God. ⁶Before the throne there was a sea of glass, like crystal. And in the midst of the throne, and around the throne, were four living creatures full of eyes in front and in back.*
>
> *⁷The first living creature was like a lion, the second living creature like a calf, the third living creature had a face like a man, and the fourth living creature was like a flying eagle. ⁸The four living creatures, each having six wings, were full of eyes around and within. And they do not rest day or night, saying: Holy, holy, holy, Lord God Almighty, Who was and is and is to come!" (Revelation 4:5-8)*

These heavenly beings are probably the cherubims or seraphims in Isaiah 6 and Ezekiel 1 and 10.

Ezekiel describes the *four living creatures* (Ezekiel 1:5) as the same beings as the cherubim.

> "*¹⁰As for the likeness of their faces, each had the face of a man; each of the four had the face of a lion on the right side, each of the four had the face of an ox on the left side, and each of the four had the face of an eagle." (Ezekiel 1:10)*

Cherubim are angelic beings involved in the worship and praise of God. They move fast, using a wheel within a wheel, and their wings cover their body.

The first mention of cherubims is in Genesis.

> "²⁴ *After He drove the man out, He placed on the east side of the Garden of Eden cherubim and a flaming sword flashing back and forth to guard the way to the tree of life."* (Genesis 3:24).

Prior to his rebellion, Satan was a cherub.

> "*^{14}You were the anointed cherub who covers; I established you; You were on the holy mountain of God; You walked back and forth in the midst of fiery stones. ^{15}You were perfect in your ways from the day you were created, Till iniquity was found in you." (Ezekiel 28:12-15)*

The main difference between the cherubim and seraphim is their appearance.

The seraphims only appear in the book of Isaiah. Their name means *burning ones or flying serpents*. Seraphim use two of their wings for flight. Like the cherubim, they are among the highest order of angelic beings.

Each creature symbolizes and represent the attributes of God. They are full of eyes within and without representing the omniscience and omnipresence of God. They are likened to a lion, ox, man, and eagle. Each representing different aspects of God's attributes.

- Lion: King of Beasts, majesty, and omnipotence.
- Ox: Patience and continuous labor.
- Man: Intelligence and rational power.
- Eagle: Sovereignty and supremacy, the greatest of birds.

Now for the beginning of the Tribulation.

Chapter 8

Daniel, Matthew, and Revelation Part 2 Tribulation

The Tribulation Defined

Daniel 9:24-27 describes a period of seventy weeks which predict the future of the nation of Israel and the Jewish people. It also predicts the first coming and crucifixion of their Messiah, the subsequent coming of the Antichrist to stage the *abomination of desolation*, and the coming destruction of the Temple and Jerusalem.

From the previous chapter on the 70 weeks of Daniel, 69 weeks were completed when Jesus was crucified. A *gap* exists between the 69th and the 70th week. This gap can be compared to a prophetic clock that has stopped.

Why did God stop the prophetic clock?

The Talmud - the book of Jewish civil and ceremonial law is divided into three main periods of God's timeline for humanity before the start of the Millennium:

- The first 2,000 years were before the Torah – the time before Abraham.
- The second 2,000 years of the Torah – the time from Abraham to Jesus.

- The third 2,000 years of their Messiah – the period from Jesus to the Rapture of the Church.

God paused or stopped the clock after the 69th week. If the 70th week started immediately after Jesus was crucified, the end of the age would have occurred. Then God's promise to Abraham to bless *"all the families of the earth"* would not have been kept.

Therefore, the 2,000 years of the Messiah described in the Talmud is now called the *Church Age*. It is the time God extends grace to the Gentiles (and Jews) to accept Jesus as their Savior or Messiah.

The 6,000 years is nearly up and we are waiting to restart the clock on the 70th week. The final week starts after the Rapture and ends after seven years when the Battle of Armageddon is finished.

The seven year Tribulation will provide all non-believers one last opportunity to repent of their sins and accept Jesus as their Savior. God provides excruciating details about the Tribulation because He wants everyone to avoid going through the Tribulation. All they have to do is accept Jesus as their Savior. To help people make this decision, God inspired both Old and New Testament authors of books in the Bible to graphically describe the Tribulation.

The Tribulation also sets the stage for the elimination of Satan, the Antichrist, and all of Israel's enemies.

What does *abomination of desolation* mean?

The phrase *abomination of desolation* means an idolatrous image or an act of pagan sacrilege is performed within the Temple sanctuary. This act produces the highest level of ceremonial impurity or blasphemous action possible. An abomination is something that God loathes or hates because it is offensive to Him and His character.

In the middle of the 70th week, or after three and one half years, a very distinct event occurs. It is described in detail in Daniel, Matthew, and Revelation as *the abomination of desolation*. The intensity of the judgments increases dramatically after this. Therefore, the first half of this period is called the *Lesser Tribulation* and the last half, as the *Great Tribulation*.

The importance of this event cannot be overstated. It is the beginning of the most terrible span of time in human existence. Words cannot adequately describe the agony and pain the remaining people on earth will go through.

The following descriptions follow a pattern describing how the three primary authors on the Tribulation describe the same event. At the conclusion of these comparisons, a sampling from scores of similar prophecies about the Tribulation are presented. This type of format lets you compare how similar the descriptions are.

Daniel - *Abomination of Desolation*

Daniel 9:27 reveals several key prophecies. The Antichrist breaks the seven year peace agreement or covenant with Israel in the middle of its term. Then he stops the Jews from offering sacrifices and exalts himself as the Prince most high (God) and changes the worship laws of the Jews. Both Matthew and Revelation reinforce Daniel's statements. It is clear these actions are an abomination to God and the Jews.

> "[27]*Then he shall confirm a covenant with many for one week; <u>But in the middle of the week He shall bring an end to sacrifice and offering</u>. And on the wing of abominations shall be one who makes desolate, Even until the*

> *consummation, which is determined, Is poured out on the desolate." (Daniel 9:27)*
>
> *"[25]He shall <u>speak pompous words against the Most High</u>, Shall <u>persecute the saints</u> of the Most High, And shall intend to change times and law. Then the saints shall be given into his hand for a time and times and half a time." (Daniel 7:25)*
>
> *"[11]He even exalted himself as high as the Prince of the host; and by him the daily sacrifices were taken away, and the place of His sanctuary was cast down." (Daniel 8:11)*

The *he* mentioned in Daniel 9:27 is the *prince who is to come* or the Antichrist who empowers the false prophet to create *the abomination of desolation.*

Matthew - *Abomination of Desolation*

Jesus' disciples asked when the end of the age would occur and when He would return. Jesus thought it was important to specifically answer their questions. Therefore, He used Old Testament scriptures every Jew in His day knew from the book of Daniel.

> *"[15]Therefore when you see the <u>abomination of desolation</u>, spoken of by Daniel the prophet, standing in the holy place (whoever reads, let him understand), [16]then let those who are in Judea flee to the mountains. [17]Let him who is on the housetop not go down to take anything out of his house. [18]And let him who is in the field not go back to get his clothes." (Matthew 24:15-18)*

Revelation - *Abomination of Desolation*

Some seventy years after the death of Jesus, God revealed the same events to the Apostle John. God expanded on Daniel's vision which John recorded in detail in the book of Revelation.

Revelation 6 confirms the prophecies in Daniel and Jesus spoke of by describing the abomination, triggering the *Great Tribulation* which is the last half of the Tribulation.

> "*⁵And he was given a mouth speaking great things and blasphemies, and he was given authority to continue for <u>forty-two months</u>. ⁶Then he opened his mouth in blasphemy against God, to blaspheme His name, His tabernacle, and those who dwell in heaven." (Revelation 13:5-6)*

> "*¹³And I saw three unclean spirits like frogs coming out of the mouth of the dragon, out of the mouth of the beast, and out of the mouth of the false prophet." (Revelation 16:13)*

Here is an additional New Testament reference describing the *abomination of desolation in succinct terms.*

> "*³…that Day will not come unless the falling away comes first, and the man of sin is revealed, the son of perdition, ⁴who opposes and exalts himself above all that is called God or that is worshiped, so that he sits as God in the temple of God, showing himself that he is God." (2 Thessalonians 2:3-4).*

Mark of the Beast - 666

After the *abomination of desolation*, one of the Antichrist's first actions of his new one-world religious order will be to *"change times and laws"* (Daniel 7:25). This means abolishing God's Sabbath, holy days, and all Biblical laws. Those who fail to comply will be persecuted for refusing to turn away from God's laws. This will be particularly offensive to all Jews. When the Antichrist declares himself to be God, people must choose to take the mark of the beast and follow his religious system. If they don't, they will die.

> "*[25]He shall speak pompous words against the Most High, Shall persecute the saints of the Most High, And shall intend to change times and law. Then the saints shall be given into his hand for a time and times and half a time." (Daniel 9:25)*

> "*[27]Then he shall confirm a covenant with many for one week; But in the middle of the week He shall bring an end to sacrifice and offering. And on the wing of abominations shall be one who makes desolate, Even until the consummation, which is determined, Is poured out on the desolate." (Daniel 9:27)*

The proverbial *line in the sand* is drawn. If you fail to make the Rapture, which side of the line will you stand on? Not only does your physical life on earth depend upon this decision, but so does your eternal life. Heaven or Hell! Think about it.

What role does the false prophet or the second beast of Revelation play in the End Times?

> "*[11]Then I saw another beast coming up out of the earth, and he had two horns like a lamb and spoke like a dragon. [12]And he exercises all the authority of the first beast in his presence, and causes the earth and those who dwell in it to worship the first beast, whose deadly wound was healed. [13]He performs great signs, so that he even makes fire come down from heaven on the earth in the sight of men." (Revelation 13:11-15)*

The false prophet rises out the earth from the pits of hell. He is empowered by the Antichrist with all the demonic powers of hell at his command. The beast or false prophet possesses the ability to perform signs and deceive.

> *"^{13}And I saw three unclean spirits like frogs coming out of the mouth of the dragon, out of the mouth of the beast, and out of the mouth of the false prophet. ^{14}For they are spirits of demons, performing signs, which go out to the kings of the earth and of the whole world."* (Revelation16:13-14)

Unlike the Antichrist beast with heads and horns representing power and might, the false prophet uses gentle and persuasive words that elicit sympathy and good will from others. He is an extraordinary preacher or orator whose demonically empowered words deceive the multitudes. He rises to a prominent position as a world religious leader. He displays miraculous signs and wonders to deceive people into willingly worshipping the Antichrist. He deceives the people to worship the Antichrist.

Next, we will examine prophecies about the coming Millennial Kingdom.

Chapter 9

Daniel, Matthew, and Revelation – Part 3 The Coming Kingdom

The Millennium and Eternal Kingdom Prophesied

Daniel – God's Coming Kingdom

Daniel clearly predicts the coming kingdom which *"shall not be destroyed."*

> *"[13]I was watching in the night visions, and behold, One like the Son of Man, coming with the clouds of heaven. He came to the Ancient of Days, and they brought Him near before Him. [14]Then to Him was given dominion and glory and a kingdom, that all peoples, nations and languages should serve Him. <u>His dominion is an everlasting dominion, which shall not pass away, and His kingdom the one which shall not be destroyed</u>." (Daniel 7:13-14)*

Daniel 11:36-45 describes the destruction of the Antichrist. Daniel 12 describes the deliverance of Israel which precedes the coming kingdom of Jesus.

> *"[13]But you, go your way till the end; for you shall rest, and will arise to your inheritance at the end of the days." (Daniel 12:13)*

Matthew – God's Coming Kingdom

Jesus was asked by His disciples in Matthew 24:3 about *"the sign of Your coming, and of the end of the age."* Whenever you see *"end of the age"*, it means the end of the current era, *Church Age,* we are in. It simultaneously signals the beginning of the reign of Jesus on earth in the Millennium.

Jesus proceeds to tell them the signs that will happen before the Rapture and the first half of the Tribulation.

> *"⁴And Jesus answered and said to them: Take heed that no one deceives you. ⁵For many will come in My name, saying, I am the Christ, and will deceive many. ⁶And you will hear of wars and rumors of wars. See that you are not troubled; for all these things must come to pass, but the end is not yet. ⁷For nation will rise against nation, and kingdom against kingdom. And there will be famines, pestilences, and earthquakes in various places. ⁸All these are the beginning of sorrows.*
>
> *⁹Then they will deliver you up to tribulation and kill you, and you will be hated by all nations for My name's sake. ¹⁰And then many will be offended, will betray one another, and will hate one another. ¹¹Then many false prophets will rise up and deceive many. ¹²And because lawlessness will abound, the love of many will grow cold. ¹³But he who endures to the end shall be saved. ¹⁴And this gospel of the kingdom will be preached in all the world as a witness to all the nations, and then the end will come." (Matthew 24:4-14)*

Jesus then describes the second half of the Tribulation in verses (Matthew 24:15-26). Then He describes the Second Coming and His future kingdom.

> "²⁷For as the lightning comes from the east and flashes to the west, so also will the coming of the Son of Man be. ²⁸For wherever the carcass is, there the eagles will be gathered together. ²⁹Immediately after the tribulation of those days the sun will be darkened, and the moon will not give its light; the stars will fall from heaven, and the powers of the heavens will be shaken.
>
> ³⁰And at that time the sign of the Son of Man [coming in His glory] will appear in the sky, and then all the tribes of the earth [and especially Israel] will mourn [regretting their rebellion and rejection of the Messiah], and they will see the Son of Man coming on the clouds of heaven with power and great glory [in brilliance and splendor]." (Matthew 24:27-30)

Here are additional references to His Second Coming.

> "³¹When the Son of Man comes in His glory, and all the holy angels with Him, then He will sit on the throne of His glory. ³²All the nations will be gathered before Him, and He will separate them one from another, as a shepherd divides his sheep from the goats." (Matthew 25:31-32)
>
> "²⁸So Jesus said to them, Assuredly I say to you, that in the regeneration, when the Son of Man sits on the throne of His glory, you who have followed Me will also sit on twelve thrones, judging the twelve tribes of Israel." (Matthew 19:28)

Jesus also used parables in Matthew to describe the coming kingdom: the marriage feast or great banquet (Matthew 22:1-14), the budding fig tree (Matthew 24:32-35), the faithful servant versus the wicked servant (Matthew 34:45-51), the ten virgins (Matthew 25:1-13), and the ten talents (Matthew 25:14-30).

Revelation – God's Coming Kingdom

After defeating Satan, the Millennial reign of Jesus will begin for 1,000 years.

> "[15]Then the seventh angel sounded: And there were loud voices in heaven, saying, <u>The kingdoms of this world have become the kingdoms of our Lord and of His Christ, and He shall reign forever and ever!</u>" (Revelation 11:15)

> "[4]And I saw thrones, and they sat on them, and judgment was committed to them. Then I saw the souls of those who had been beheaded for their witness to Jesus and for the word of God, who had not worshiped the beast or his image, and had not received his mark on their foreheads or on their hands. <u>And they lived and reigned with Christ for a thousand years</u>. [5]But the rest of the dead did not live again until the thousand years were finished." (Revelation 20:4-6)

Next, we will examine the prophecies in Revelation with an emphasis on Tribulation scriptures.

Chapter 10

Revelation Summary

Revelation is an inspired book of God predicting future events affecting real people. God inspired the Apostle John to transcribe His words into what we know as the book of Revelation.

Every individual who is alive or has died will be a participant in the future events described before the Millennium and Eternity begins. Since each reader of these pages must inevitably participate in some of these future events, even if you don't want to, my goal is to explain Revelation in simple terms so the events are clear and you can understand them.

Revelation contains some of most important events since the resurrection of Jesus. It is essential we understand them so we can plan to avoid them!

Revelation was written specifically to provide knowledge of the future. This is made clear in the very first verse:

> "[1]*The Revelation of Jesus Christ, which God gave Him to show His servants - things which must shortly take place. And He sent and signified it by His angel to His servant John, [2]who bore witness to the word of God, and to the testimony of Jesus Christ, to all things that he saw."* (Revelation 1:1)

We should not wonder if the prophecies in Revelation will be filled. Unlike the false prophets of both past and present, **God's prophecies are true and will come to pass.**

> "[19]*And so we have the prophetic word confirmed, which you do well to heed as a light that shines in a dark place, until the day dawns and the morning star rises in your hearts;* [20]*knowing this first, that no prophecy of Scripture is of any private interpretation,* [21]*for prophecy never came by the will of man, but holy men of God spoke as they were moved by the Holy Spirit." (2 Peter 1:19-21)*

The Book of Revelation is the final word from God. It contains references to both Old and New Testament prophecies. Many have been completed, yet some remain unfulfilled. Unfortunately, Revelation is not understood by most Christians. It contains symbolism which requires study to understand it. Perhaps this why those who read and study Revelation are blessed. When it is read and studied, mysteriously a light goes on inside your head. Then you see the messages in Revelation clearly.

> "[3]*Blessed is he who reads and those who hear the words of this prophecy, and keep those things which are written in it; for the time is near." (Revelation 1:3)*

While studying Revelation, it becomes apparent God is destroying the forces of Satan. When the destruction is completed, God can fulfill the unconditional promises He made to Abraham, the Jews, King David, and to the nation of Israel. Let me give you an example to encourage you to learn symbols needed to understand Revelation.

There is a natural phenomenon of learning that comes from repetition. If you repeat a difficult task often enough, you will master it so it becomes easier to do, e.g., playing a musical instrument or sports. Reading the Bible for understanding can be difficult unless you spend time studying it. When you study the Bible, it comes to life. Then you begin to understand God and your faith comes alive because you start seeing God is faithful and that He always completes His promises. Then, if you think on all the promises and predictions God has fulfilled, your faith will increase. Faith causes hope to arise.

Increasing faith in God is the best way to become victorious in this life we live. Faith is the vehicle you use to drive through the many tests and trials of life.

> "*[6]...without faith it is impossible to please Him, for he who comes to God must believe He is, and that He is a rewarder of those who diligently seek Him." (Hebrews 11:6)*

By faith, we overcome all trials in this life and have a great reward at the end of our journey.

> "*[11]And they overcame him by the blood of the Lamb and by the word of their testimony, and they did not love their lives to the death." (Revelation 12:11)*

Exercising faith by believing you will ascend to meet Jesus in the Rapture also makes it easier for you to keep watching for the Rapture. You don't want to miss it!

A study of Revelation should provide you to the incentive to keep watching for it.

Let me start with an outline of Revelation.

1. Chapters 1- 3: describe the 2,000 years of the Church Age. It begins with the start of Jesus' ministry and continues until the Rapture.
2. Chapters 4 – 19: describe the seven years of Tribulation plagues and judgments.

3. Chapter 20: provides insight into the 1,000 year Millennial Kingdom Jesus establishes.
4. Chapters 21 – 22: Describe the Millennium and Eternity.

From the outline, you can see the bulk of the book of Revelation explains the seven years of Tribulation.

A short summary of Revelation follows. However, to fully appreciate the depth of Revelation, a full study is needed.

There are two divisions of time in the Tribulation. The first division encompasses the first three and one half years and is called the *Lesser Tribulation*, for it is not as great in severity as the last half. Israel conducts Temple worship and performs sacrifices for the first half of the Tribulation. They escape the wars in the rest of the world because of their peace agreement with the Antichrist.

The second division, or the last three and one half years, which is called *The Great Tribulation* because severe persecution comes upon Israel and the rest of the world. It is also referred to as the *Time of Jacob's Troubles*. The Antichrist breaks the peace agreement with Israel in the middle of the seven years. The Antichrist takes over the Temple the Jews have rebuilt in an act described as the *abomination of desolation.* The Antichrist declares he is God and demands the Jews worship him. They must take the mark of the beast, 666 or die. The Jews refuse and flee from Jerusalem.

The last three and one half years is the time of extreme testing for the Jews. The persecution they endure becomes intense as their period of rebellion against their Messiah Jesus is coming to an end.

Chapter 1: John gives a graphic description of Jesus and describes His majesty. John describes how Jesus comes in the clouds and every eye will see Him including those who pierced

Him. This is a reference to Jesus' second coming at the end of the Tribulation when the Jews exclaim, He is the Messiah.

Chapters 2 and 3: The letters to the seven churches describe what Jesus wants the Church to become and the corrections they need to make to become a better Church. These instructions enable the Church to be filled with believers who are overcomers of all the trials and tests in this world.

Chapters 4 and 5: Jesus is deemed to be worthy to take the scroll with the seven seals and open it. The seals start the judgments that display the power of God to convict humanity of their sins, destroy the evil nations of the world, and cast Satan into the lake of fire.

Chapter 6 - 22: These chapters describe how God prepares the nations for the transition of all governments into the Kingdom of God. God's wrath is poured out on the Antichrist's world empire in the *three numbered judgment series*: seven seals, seven trumpets, and seven bowls. They are connected to one another. The seventh seal introduces the seven trumpets (Revelation 8:1–5), and the seventh trumpet introduces the seven bowls (Revelation 11:15–19; 15:1–8). They are numbered so they occur in a sequential order.

<u>These judgments are literal and actual events</u>. They are not to be explained away symbolically. They will occur in the future. They progressively increase in intensity and severity until the end of the Tribulation.

Jesus, as the Lamb of God, will initiate the release of the seven seals by opening a sealed scroll.

> *"[5]Then one of the elders said to me, Do not weep! See, the Lion of the tribe of Judah, the Root of David, has triumphed. He is able to open the scroll and its seven seals." (Revelation 5:5)*

The first six seals are all opened in Revelation 6. The seventh seal is opened in Chapter 8 and continues through much of the rest of the book. The seventh seal represents the Day of the Lord and is actually the main theme of the book. The Day of the Lord is the time of Jesus' intervention in this world to take control from Satan and from the rebellious human rulers under him. At the end of this Day, Jesus establishes the Kingdom of God here on Earth.

An important point to realize is that once each seal is opened, it remains open! In other words, each seal is added to the seals previously opened and taking their toll. They all greatly intensify as the end of this world draws near.

When the first four seals are opened, the four horsemen of the Apocalypse are sent out to create war, bring disease, famine and pestilence. Their activities kill millions.

The scroll's fifth seal reveals those who have been martyred for their faith in Jesus during the Tribulation (Revelation 6:9–11). The souls of these martyrs are pictured as dwelling under the altar in heaven crying out to God to give them vengeance. God hears their cries for justice, and He gives each of them a white robe. The martyrs are told to wait and God promises to avenge them. But the time has not yet come (Revelation 6:16-17).

When the Lamb of God opens the sixth seal, a devastating earthquake occurs, causing massive upheaval and terrible devastation, along with unusual astronomical phenomena: the sun turns black, and the moon turns blood-red, and *the heavens receded like a scroll being rolled up, and every mountain and island was removed from its place"* (Revelation 6:12–14).

Survivors of the sixth seal, regardless of their social position, take refuge in caves and cry out to the mountains and the rocks:

> "*[16]Fall on us and hide us from the face of him who sits on the throne and from the wrath of the Lamb! For the great day of their wrath has come, and who can stand?" (Revelation 6:16).*

These supernatural events had long before been foretold as signs announcing the Day of the Lord by the prophet Joel.

> "*[1]...For the day of the Lord is coming, For it is at hand: [2]A day of darkness and gloominess, A day of clouds and thick darkness." (Joel 2:1-22)*

> "*[15]The sun and moon will grow dark, And the stars will diminish their brightness. [16]The Lord also will roar from Zion, and utter His voice from Jerusalem; The heavens and earth will shake; But the Lord will be a shelter for His people, And the strength of the children of Israel." (Joel 3:15-16)*

As these awesome events occur, mankind realizes that God is bringing punishment on them because of disobedience to His laws.

> "*[15]And the kings of the earth, the great men, the rich men, the commanders, the mighty men, every slave and every free man, hid themselves in the caves and in the rocks of the mountains, [16]and said to the mountains and rocks, Fall on us and hide us from the face of Him who sits on the throne and from the wrath of the Lamb! [17]For the great day of His wrath has come, and who is able to stand?" (Revelation 6:15-17)*

The seventh seal begins with a sequence of seven trumpets. (Revelation 8:7). The *Day of the Lord* begins when this seal is opened. It represents *"the wrath of the Lamb"* which Jesus brings upon humanity because of disobedience to God's laws. It also represents the mercy of God when Jesus returns to establish the Kingdom of God (Revelation 6:16).

As the seventh seal begins, seven trumpets blast away, representing a series of punishments coming in the next set of judgments (Revelation 8:6).

The trumpet judgments are supernatural acts of God through nature (the first four trumpets) and demons (the fifth and sixth trumpets). The ten plagues of Egypt (Ezekiel 7–12) are appearing again in the trumpets and bowls of wrath, but they extend to the whole world instead of just Egypt. God warned Israel that He would judge their rebellion with the Egyptian plagues (Deuteronomy 28:27–60).

Some of the judgments and plagues in Revelation are like the Egyptian plagues used to convince Pharaoh to let the Jewish people return to the *Promised Land*. Moses repeatedly stated to Pharaoh, *"Let my people go."* The plagues in Revelation are to convince the non-believers to turn to Jesus as their Savior. An analogy could be God declaring to the non-believers, *"Let go of your sin and return to Me."* Unfortunately, the message falls mostly on deaf ears, and people are destroyed just like Pharaoh was.

The first five trumpets in Revelation 8 parallel five of the plagues of Egypt. The first trumpet (verse 7) parallels the seventh plague of fire mingled with blood (Exodus 9:22-26). The second and third trumpets (verses 8–11) parallel the first plague of the Nile turning to blood (Exodus 7:19–25). The fourth trumpet (verse 12) parallels the ninth plague of darkness (Exodus 10:21–23). The fifth trumpet (Revelation 9:1-11) parallels the eighth plague of locusts tormenting the people (Exodus 10:12–20).

By the time of the fifth trumpet, the punishments are severe.

> "*⁶...men will seek death and will not find it; they will desire to die, and death will flee from them*" (Revelation 9:6)

During the sixth trumpet, a third of mankind is killed.

> "*¹⁵So the four angels, who had been prepared for the hour and day and month and year, were released to kill a third of mankind. ¹⁶Now the number of the army of the horsemen was two hundred million; I heard the number of them. ¹⁷And thus I saw the horses in the vision: those who sat on them had breastplates of fiery red, hyacinth blue, and sulfur yellow; and the heads of the horses were like the heads of lions; and out of their mouths came fire, smoke, and brimstone. ¹⁸By these three plagues a third of mankind was killed - by the fire and the smoke and the brimstone which came out of their mouths.*" (Revelation 9:15-18)

The seventh trumpet announces that *"the kingdoms of this world have become the kingdoms of our Lord and of His Christ"* (Revelation 11:15). The seventh trumpet announces the seven last plagues, also called *"bowls full of the wrath of God."*

> "*¹Then I saw another sign in heaven, great and marvelous: seven angels having the seven last plagues, for in them the wrath of God is complete.*" (Revelation 15:1)

The seven bowl or vial judgments are the final judgments of the Tribulation period. They are the most severe judgments the world has experienced. The seven bowls are described in Revelation 16:1–21, where they are specifically called *"the seven bowls of God's wrath."* Under the Antichrist, the wickedness of man has reached its peak, and it is met with

God's wrath against sin. The seven bowl judgments are called forth by the seventh trumpet.

The first bowl causes sores or boils on those who have taken the mark of the beast. Anyone who has not taken the mark does not receive any boils.

> "*²a foul and loathsome sore came upon the men who had the mark of the beast and those who worshiped his image (Revelation 16:2).*

The second bowl is poured out on the sea, and the water *"became blood as of a dead man; and every living creature in the sea died"* (Revelation 16:3).

A third of the sea life had already perished with the sounding of the second trumpet (Revelation 8:9), and now the rest of the sea life is gone. The oceans are dead.

The third bowl also causes the rivers and freshwater springs to turn into blood (Revelation 16:4-5).

The fourth bowl is poured out on the sun:

> "*⁸...poured out his bowl on the sun, and power was given to him to scorch men with fire. ⁹And men were scorched with great heat, and they blasphemed the name of God who has power over these plagues; and they did not repent and give Him glory." (Revelation 16:8–9)*

The fifth bowl causes the kingdom of the beast to be plunged into great darkness. The pain and suffering of the wicked intensify, so that people gnaw their tongues in agony. Still, the followers of the Antichrist *"refused to repent of what they had done"* (Revelation 16:10-11).

The sixth bowl dries up the Euphrates River. That river is dried up in preparation for the "kings of the East" to cross over it to meet their destruction at Armageddon. John then sees three unclean spirits *"that looked like frogs"* coming from the mouths of Satan, the Antichrist, and the false prophet. These demons perform miracles and deceive the kings of the earth and gather them to the final battle on the Day of the Lord. Under demonic influence, *"the kings [gather] together to the place that in Hebrew is called Armageddon"* (Revelation 16:12-16).

The seventh bowl is emptied into the atmosphere. A loud voice in heaven says, **"It is done!"** The seventh bowl results in flashes of lightning and an earthquake so severe that *"no earthquake like it has ever occurred since mankind has been on earth, so tremendous was the quake"*. Jerusalem is split into three parts, and the cities of the world collapse. Islands are flooded, and mountains disappear. Giant hailstones, *"each weighing about a hundred pounds, fell on people"*. Those under judgment *"cursed God on account of the plague of hail, because the plague was so terrible"* (Revelation 16:17-21).

In Revelation Chapters 17 and 18, one of the angels of the seven bowl judgments shows John the fate of the great harlot of Babylon. The term harlot is used throughout the Old Testament as a metaphor for false religion. The harlot is neither the Antichrist nor the false prophet. The harlot refers to another person, possibly persons, in charge of this religious institution. The actual identity and makeup of the religion has been debated for centuries. A number of different views among Bible commentators and theologians exist. Some believe this religious institution comes from Catholicism, Islam, the New Age movement, or some form of religion not even yet invented.

The false prophet establishes a one-world religious system which is made up of a number of different religions combined into one. The religion or church will be controlled by the harlot. The harlot makes the religious system look and function like a church, but the harlot has the power to enforce its set of beliefs as if they are civil laws by invoking punishment upon disobedient members.

We are provided with several characteristics of the one-world religion. The false religion dominates all the *"peoples and multitudes and nations and tongues"* of the earth (Revelation 17:15). This domination comes with universal authority which has been given to the harlot from the Antichrist to rule the world at that time.

Previously, the demise of the harlot was described, so it will not be repeated again. God avenges *"the blood of prophets and of God's holy people, of all who have been slaughtered on the earth"* (Revelation 18:24) by destroying the harlot. The world mourns the fall of Babylon (Chapter 18), but Heaven rejoices (Chapter 19). Please note the destruction of the harlot occurs before the Battle of Armageddon.

Jesus Christ then returns in glory to defeat the armies of the Antichrist at Armageddon (Revelation 19:11–21) and to set up His kingdom on Earth (Revelation 20:1–6).

The Second Coming of Jesus will take place during the events described during the seventh bowl, or soon thereafter.

Wow! That was a lot to absorb and comprehend. Do you feel overwhelmed that this is too complicated to remember all these judgments? To give you a resource and study guide, the table below presents a summary of each judgment. It is designed to jog your memory if you can't remember the types of judgments or their consequences.

Revelation and Daniel Reveal How and When the World Ends

Type of Judgment	Plague	Revelation Chapter: Verse
SEAL		
# of Seal		
1	White horse - sent out to conquer	6:1-2
2	Red horse - sent to wage war, and kill	6:3-4
3	Black horse - brings famine and economic collapse	6:5-6
4	Pale horse - brings disease and death to 1/4 of earth	6:8
5	Cry of martyrs to avenge their deaths	6:9-11
6	Earthquake, skies blacken, meteorite storm	6:12-17
7	Fire from heaven falls, Call for Trumpets to begin	8:1-4
TRUMPET		
# of Trumpet		
1	Hail and fire destroy 1/3 of trees and plants	8:7
2	Mountain burning with fire falls into sea - 1/3 of fish, ships destroyed, sea turns to blood	8:8
3	1/3 of earth's fresh water destroyed	8:10-11
4	1/3 of Sun, moon, stars darkened	8:12
5	Demonic locusts torment for 5 months	9:1-12
6	Demonic horsemen kill 1/3 of mankind	9:13-21
7	Calls for bowl judgments to begin	11:15
BOWLS or VIALS		
1	Boils/sores come on those with Mark of Beast	16:2
2	Sea turns to blood and everything in it dies	16:3
3	Water in rivers, springs become blood	16:4-6
4	Sun scorches people with heat	16:8-9
5	Total darkness comes on earth	16:10-11
6	Three demons go to get kings to come to Battle of Armageddon	16:12-16
7	Second Coming, Armageddon, Judgement	19 and 20

Chapter 11

Revelation – The Reasons for the Judgments

The Wrath of God

The seven bowls bring the wrath of God. God's wrath is called the *Day of the Lord*.

God's wrath will be necessary to destroy the infrastructure put in place by evil leaders. God exhibits His wrath by using His power to defeat Satan.

The Day of the Lord is a day of:

- Darkness and gloominess (Joel 2:1-11)
- Punishment for the living wicked (Isaiah 1:24-31)
- Trouble and distress (Zephaniah 1:7-18)
- Dreadful day (Joel 2:31)
- God's wrath poured out upon the enemies of Israel (Isaiah 13:6-9)
- Destruction for the wicked people on earth (2 Thessalonians 1:6-10)

God's Reasons for Bringing the Plagues

God had an intricate master plan that repeatedly used prophetic declarations throughout the Bible to describe His plans for the redemption of humanity. God tells us in advance when humanity's 6,000 year lease to rule the earth ends. He explains why it is going to happen, and what we can expect in the Millennium and Eternity. Here is a partial list of scripture depicting some of the reasons for Revelation, the judgements, and the final outcome.

1. Judge the living nations.

    "*[32]All the nations will be gathered before Him, and He will separate them one from another, as a shepherd divides his sheep from the goats." (Matthew 25:32)*

2. Bring salvation to Israel.

    "*[26]And so all Israel will be saved, as it is written:
    The Deliverer will come out of Zion,
    And He will turn away ungodliness from Jacob;
    [27]For this is My covenant with them,
    When I take away their sins." (Romans 11:26-27)*

3. Destroy the lawless one.

    "*[7]For the mystery of lawlessness is already at work; only He who now restrains will do so until He is taken out of the way. [8]And then the lawless one will be revealed, whom the Lord will consume with the breath of His mouth and destroy with the brightness of His coming." (2 Thessalonians 7-8)*

4. Deliver creation from bondage.

    [20]For the creation was subjected to futility, not willingly, but because of Him who subjected it in hope; [21]because the creation itself also will be delivered from the bondage

of corruption into the glorious liberty of the children of God." (Romans 8:20-21)*

5. Reestablish David's throne and kingdom.

   *"^{15}And with this the words of the prophets agree, just as it is written: ^{16}After this I will return and will rebuild the tabernacle of David, which has fallen down;
   I will rebuild its ruins, And I will set it up; ^{17}So that the rest of mankind may seek the Lord.
   Even all the Gentiles who are called by My name, Says the Lord who does all these things." (Acts 15:15-17)*

6. Execute righteousness and justice on earth.

   *"^{5}Behold, the days are coming, says the Lord,
   That I will raise to David a Branch of righteousness;
   A King shall reign and prosper,
   And execute judgment and righteousness in the earth.
   ^{6}In His days Judah will be saved,
   And Israel will dwell safely;
   Now this is His name by which He will be called:
   THE LORD OUR RIGHTEOUSNESS." (Jeremiah 23:5-6)*

7. Reign over all nations.

   "^{15}Then the seventh angel sounded: And there were loud voices in heaven, saying, The kingdoms of this world have become the kingdoms of our Lord and of His Christ, and He shall reign forever and ever!" (Revelation 11:15)

8. Establish the raptured saints as kings and priests.

"⁹And they sang a new song, saying: You are worthy to take the scroll,
And to open its seals; For You were slain, And have redeemed us to God by Your blood
Out of every tribe and tongue and people and nation, ¹⁰And have made us kings and priests to our God; And we shall reign on the earth." (Revelation 5:9-10)

9. Regather all Israel completely.

"³⁰Then the sign of the Son of Man will appear in heaven, and then all the tribes of the earth will mourn, and they will see the Son of Man coming on the clouds of heaven with power and great glory. ³¹And He will send His angels with a great sound of a trumpet, and they will gather together His elect from the four winds, from one end of heaven to the other." (Matthew 24:30-31)

10. Put down all rebellion on Earth.

"²⁴Then comes the end, when He delivers the kingdom to God the Father, when He puts an end to all rule and all authority and power. ²⁵For He must reign till He has put all enemies under His feet. ²⁶The last enemy that will be destroyed is death. ²⁷For He has put all things under His feet. But when He says all things are put under Him, it is evident that He who put all things under Him is excepted. ²⁸Now when all things are made subject to Him, then the Son Himself will also be subject to Him who put all things under Him, that God may be all in all." (1 Corinthians 15:24-28)

11. Build the Jewish Millennial temple.

   "*⁶Then I heard Him speaking to me from the temple, while a man stood beside me. ⁷And He said to me, Son of man, this is the place of My throne and the place of the soles of My feet, where I will dwell in the midst of the children of Israel forever." (Ezekiel 43:6-7)*

12. Establish God's glory on Earth.

   "*³¹When the Son of Man comes in His glory, and all the holy angels with Him, then He will sit on the throne of His glory." (Matthew 25:31)*

13. Remove every curse from the Earth.

   "*¹And he showed me a pure river of water of life, clear as crystal, proceeding from the throne of God and of the Lamb. ²In the middle of its street, and on either side of the river, was the tree of life, which bore twelve fruits, each tree yielding its fruit every month. The leaves of the tree were for the healing of the nations. ³And there shall be no more curse, but the throne of God and of the Lamb shall be in it, and His servants shall serve Him." (Revelation 22:1-3)*

14. Bring universal peace and prosperity.

   "*²For out of Zion shall go forth the law, And the word of the Lord from Jerusalem. ⁴He shall judge between the nations, And rebuke many people; They shall beat their swords into plowshares, and their spears into pruning hooks; Nation shall not lift up sword against nation, Neither shall they learn war anymore." (Isaiah 2:2-4)*

This completes the descriptions of the reasons for the plagues and judgments God sends to convince humanity to repent and turn to Jesus for salvation. Before we leave a summary of Revelation, a description needs to be added describing how God brings people to salvation during all the death and destruction going on in the Tribulation.

How do people receive salvation during the Tribulation?

God offers the opportunity to receive salvation to all non-believers during the seven years of Tribulation. It is also apparent millions get saved because a significant number are killed for their newfound belief in Jesus and God. Also, there will be millions of believers alive at the end of the Tribulation.

How and when **do the non-believers hear and receive the message?**

These scriptures reveal God's plan to offer salvation to the non-believers.

> "*³And I will appoint my two witnesses, and they will prophesy for 1,260 days, clothed in sackcloth. ⁴They are the two olive trees and the two lampstands, and they stand before the Lord of the earth. ⁵If anyone tries to harm them, fire comes from their mouths and devours their enemies. This is how anyone who wants to harm them must die. ⁶They have power to shut up the heavens so that it will not rain during the time they are prophesying; and they have power to turn the waters into blood and to strike the earth with every kind of plague as often as they want." (Revelation 11:3-6)*

Nowhere does the Bible identify these two witnesses by name, although people through the years have speculated, they could be Moses, Elijah, or Enoch.

The following scriptures describe the 144,000 Jews.

> "³Do not harm the land or the sea or the trees until we put a seal on the foreheads of the servants of our God. ⁴Then I heard the number of those who were sealed: 144,000 from all the tribes of Israel. Then I heard the number of those who were sealed: 144,000 from all the tribes of Israel.
>
> ⁵From the tribe of Judah 12,000 were sealed,
> from the tribe of Reuben 12,000,
> from the tribe of Gad 12,000,
> ⁶from the tribe of Asher 12,000,
> from the tribe of Naphtali 12,000,
> from the tribe of Manasseh 12,000,
> ⁷from the tribe of Simeon 12,000,
> from the tribe of Levi 12,000,
> from the tribe of Issachar 12,000,
> ⁸from the tribe of Zebulun 12,000,
> from the tribe of Joseph 12,000,
> from the tribe of Benjamin 12,000." (Revelation 7:3-8)

Another book would be needed to fully discuss the issues these scriptures generate. The first question that arises when a comparison of the Revelation list is made to the original tribes. It is different. It is also different from the tribes who were allocated land.

"Which one should be used?"

From the Revelation list, Ephraim and Dan are excluded.

"Why Dan is not on the list?"

Here are the next questions:

> *"Where are the ten lost tribes of Israel that were deported or lost after Israel's conquest by the Neo-Assyrian Empire around 722 B.C.?*
>
> *If they are lost and disbanded, where and how does God get the 12,000 from each tribe?"*

I am going to answer these questions with a famous quote that was taken from one of Charles Spurgeon's sermons, *"sometimes only God knows."* I could write several pages explaining why Dan's tribe was removed because of idolatry. I could present multiple scenarios describing folklore stories telling of God hiding the ten tribes in remote places across the world in secret places. However, at best, it would be an educated guess which does not change God's plan for using the two witnesses and the 144,000 Jews to preach salvation to all non-believers that are present during the Tribulation.

The Bible is also unclear exactly when they commence their preaching and when they appear in the Tribulation. There are cases to be presented for both at the start and at the middle of the Tribulation.

My interpretation and position are the two witnesses are empowered at the beginning of the Tribulation. At that time, there are *zero*, I repeat *zero*, believers on earth. However, God's grace and mercy still exists. God desires to give everyone in the Tribulation the opportunity to accept Jesus, so I believe they start shortly after the Rapture.

> *"[9][God] is not willing that any should perish, but that all should come to repentance."* (2 Peter 3:9).

When the two witnesses start preaching and performing signs and miracles, the 12,000 Jews from each of the twelve tribes hear and accept the message that Jesus is the true Messiah.

The 144,000 Jews become super evangelists and are dispersed around the world to offer salvation to everyone.

The two witnesses have miraculous powers to accompany their message, and no one will be able to stop them in their work. The two witnesses proclaim to the world that the disasters occurring are the judgments of God. They warn the people that these judgments are from God and eternal damnation to hell follows. They will preach the Gospel, telling the people about God's love and how Jesus died for their sins. They call for people to repent and accept Jesus by faith and declare Him to be their Lord and Savior.

The 144,000 Jews are *sealed*, which means they have the special protection from God. This keeps them safe from the plagues and from the wrath of the Antichrist.

Can you imagine 144,000 Jewish Apostles like Paul being unleased upon the lost and dying world! Millions will be saved. Their success is recorded by John.

> "*⁹After these things I looked, and behold, a great multitude which no one could number, of all nations, tribes, peoples, and tongues, standing before the throne and before the Lamb, clothed with white robes, with palm branches in their hands, ¹⁰and crying out with a loud voice, saying, Salvation belongs to our God who sits on the throne, and to the Lamb!*"

> "*¹³Then one of the elders answered, saying to me, Who are these arrayed in white robes, and where did they come from? ¹⁴And I said to him, Sir, you know. So he said to me, These are the ones who come out of the great tribulation, and washed their robes and made them white in the blood of the Lamb." (Revelation 7:9-10, 13-14)*

Loved ones of millions and millions of people will have mysteriously disappeared in the Rapture. People will be searching for answers about what is happening and why. I can only speculate, but television and social media will be used by these evangelists to rapidly dispense the message of salvation. The miracles the two witnesses perform could be live streamed over the internet. The entire world will see and hear it. Many will listen and believe their messages.

There also are hundreds of movies and thousands of books about the Rapture for people to watch and read. Multitudes will respond by accepting Jesus as their Savior.

I also believe there will be countless numbers of people saved from reading Bibles they find in their homes left behind by family members that departed in the Rapture. They will remember the testimonies from their loved ones or friends witnessing to them about Jesus. They rejected the message then as a fairy tale, but now they believe their loved ones were telling the truth about Jesus.

Also, there will be people who were "great church goers," but didn't really believe in Jesus. They will remember the sermons and come to accept Jesus as their Savior.

At the end of three and one half years, the beast kills the two witnesses and the wicked world rejoices. The bodies of the fallen prophets lie in the streets for three and a half days. Then, miraculously God's two witnesses will be resurrected and, in full view of their enemies, ascend to Heaven (Revelation 11:5-12).

Next, we are going to examine the Seven Levitical Feasts and how and when the last three will be completed. It is an amazing study to see how faithful God is to complete His promises.

Chapter 12

The Jewish Feasts in End Times Events

The following is a summary of the seven Levitical feasts. All seven feasts play a major role in God's master plan for the redemption of humanity.

Passover points to Jesus as the Passover lamb (1 Corinthians 5:7). A lamb's blood was placed over the doorposts to protect the Hebrews' firstborn from the death angel that passed through Egypt. This was the tenth and final plague before their release from Egypt. Jesus' blood serves as our covering to protect us against the justice that could be ministered against us due to our sin. In preparation for Passover, the Jews slaughtered lambs the day before Passover began. Jesus was crucified the day before Passover and He became the Passover lamb and completed this feast.

The Feast of Unleavened Bread describes Jesus' sinless life. Leaven, or yeast, is symbolic of sin throughout the Bible. Jesus was without sin and therefore he was a blameless, spotless, perfect sacrifice for our sins. Jesus' body remained in the grave during the beginning days of this feast. Like a planted seed, He resurrected into a new life. Jesus' sinless life enabled Him to fulfill this feast.

First Fruits is the first harvest celebration of the year when the Israelites were to offer the first fruits of the late spring wheat harvest. It was during this feast that Jesus came back from the dead. Therefore, Jesus became the *"first fruit"* fulfilling this feast because He defeated death and offered us new life. Paul refers to Jesus as the first fruits of the dead (1 Corinthians 15:20).

Feast of Weeks (Pentecost) involves several sacrifices tied to the theme of the harvest that was offered during the Weeks Festival. It was on Pentecost (Acts 2) that Jesus sent the Holy Spirit to the 120 believers in the Upper Room in Jerusalem. Peter preached later that day, and about 3,000 Jews accepted Jesus as their Savior. These 3,000 people became the first to receive the indwelling of the Holy Spirit. Therefore, the people became first fruits harvested with the Holy Spirit.

The birth, death, and resurrection of Jesus fulfilled the first four feasts. Please check this out and you will find this is one of the few topics Bible scholars agree on.

Hundreds of years prior to Jesus' birth Jewish customs taught that the Messiah would have differing roles within the seven feasts. A pattern of fulfillment emerges as Jesus completed the first four feasts precisely as described by the Jewish customs.

Now ask yourself:

Why would Jesus not fulfill the remaining three feasts as prophesied since he perfectly completed the first four?

What is common sense telling me?

Please note a pattern also begins emerging tying significant dates in Jesus' life to the seven Levitical feasts. Please study these feasts carefully. It becomes increasing apparent why God instructed the Jews hundreds of years in advance to celebrate each of the feasts as a rehearsal for the coming of their Messiah.

It is astonishing to see the way God fulfills the feasts He ordered the Jews to celebrate thousands of years ago!

The next three feasts are the Fall feasts that have not been fulfilled. Rosh Hashanah is the initial key for establishing the day of the Rapture.

> **Feast of Trumpets (Rosh Hashanah)** is the first fall feast. The blast of a trumpet announces the feast and the start of the new year. The trumpet reminded the Jewish people of their past, of God's power, and is a reminder for the Jewish people to remain faithful to God.
>
> For thousands of years, the feast has been associated with the coming of the Messiah in Jewish history. When the Messiah (Jesus) appears in the sky, He is returning for His Bride, the Church (1 Thessalonians 4:13–18; 1 Corinthians 15:52).
>
> After Rosh Hashanah, the *Ten Days of Awe* or *Ten Days of Repentance* begin, so the people can prepare themselves for God's judgment on Yom Kippur. People repent of their sins so they come into right standing with God during this time.
>
> **The Day of Atonement (Yom Kippur)** occurs ten days after the Feast of Trumpets. It is a day of repentance to ask God for forgiveness and to make amends. In the future, it will be a day of God's final judgment of all non-believers.
>
> Jesus' Second Coming will be on Rosh Hashanah when He touches Earth and the Battle of Armageddon will follow. When the Jewish remnant see Jesus, they will recognize Him as their Messiah. Then repentance will

occur during the ten days following, and salvation will be obtained on Yom Kippur.

> "*¹⁰look upon the One they pierced, repent of their sins, and receive Him as their Messiah." (Zechariah 12:10)*

The Feast of Tabernacles or Booths is the seventh and final festival. It foreshadows when Jesus will once again dwell with His people (Micah 4:1-7). Jesus has already come as *Immanuel, God with us*, and stayed on Earth among people. However, at His Second Coming, He will reign for 1,000 years on Earth and ultimately live with His people for all Eternity in the New Heavens and the New Earth.

When will Jesus return?

The following verses in the Bible have convinced believers for 2,000 years they cannot know when Jesus will return.

> "*³Now as He sat on the Mount of Olives, the disciples came to Him privately, saying, Tell us, when will these things be? And what will be the sign of your coming, and of the end of the age?" (Matthew 24:3)*

Jesus replied:

> "*³⁶No one knows about that day or hour, not even the angels in Heaven, nor the Son, but only the Father."* (Matthew 24:36)

In this verse, Jesus was referring to the taking home of His Bride, the Church, to Heaven. He used a familiar Jewish figure of speech or idiom referring to a specific Jewish Festival, Rosh Hashanah. "*No man knows the day or hour*" cannot be translated into English literally because it is a Jewish idiom.

The unusual fact about the Feast of Trumpets is that in the days of Jesus, **no one knew the day or hour it began**.

The Jewish festivals and weekly Shabbats for the upcoming month were sanctified for observance at the beginning of the new month by observing the moon. The celebrations were appointed times or *mo-edim* in Hebrew, which means *a sacred and set time*. From God's perspective, the appointed times belong to Him. No one has the authority to change the celebration of an appointed time.

The Sanhedrin required two witnesses to tell them when the new moon arrived. The witnesses watched for the moon to enter total darkness when there are tiny slivers of white on its edges. These are the *horns* of the moon. After correctly sighted, the *horns* determined the beginning of the new month. When the President of the Sanhedrin (who knew astronomy) was convinced their observation was accurate, he publicly sanctified the start of the new month with the blowing of the trumpets (1 Thessalonians 4:16).

Commencing on the first day of the month posed a unique problem for this feast. The first day of Tishri was the appointed time for Rosh Hashanah, the Feast of Trumpets (Leviticus 23:24). However, no one could begin observing the festival until they heard from the President of the Sanhedrin, it was "Sanctified!"

No one could start the celebration beforehand!

Thus, we can more clearly see the analogy Jesus made with His words. Jesus responded to the question, *"when are you returning,"* with an idiom that means *I am returning on the feast you have been celebrating for 1,500 years that you yourselves know nobody knows the day or the hour when it begins.*

However, you celebrate this feast as the one when the Messiah returns and brings judgment on the world!

Therefore, these words of Jesus, "*No man knows the day or hour*" has been unknowingly misinterpreted because Jesus was telling his disciples exactly the feast upon which He will return.

He will return on the Feast designed to celebrate His return for deliverance and judgment. It is the one which nobody knows the hour, or the day it begins!

The disciples and the Jews living at that time would have immediately recognized the symbolism in the phrase *"no man knows the hour or day"* to mean the Feast of Trumpets or Rosh Hashanah.

The symbolism in Jesus' words is clearly one of the *hidden mysteries* within the Bible. Unless Gentile believers are taught Jewish customs and idioms, they will miss the meaning. *How and When the World Ends*, Book 1 of this series includes a much deeper discussion on this scripture and Rosh Hashanah.

The next chapter will describe this secret, the Rapture.

Chapter 13

The Rapture and the Marriage Supper of the Lamb

The Secret of the Rapture

The Rapture of the Church is when Jesus comes to claim His bride, the Church, and take her to the Father's house which has been prepared for the bride. The Rapture occurs when Jesus appears in the clouds and calls up the body of believers to meet Him in the sky.

> "^{51}Behold, I tell you a mystery [secret]; we will not all sleep, but we will all be changed, ^{52}in a moment, in the twinkling of an eye, at the last trumpet; for the trumpet will sound, and the dead will be raised imperishable, and we will be changed. ^{53}For this perishable must put on the imperishable, and this mortal must put on immortality." (1 Corinthians 15:51-53 NASB)

God chose to reveal the *"mystery"*, or the more appropriate translation is *secret*, of the Rapture to the Apostle Paul. This *secret* had not been revealed to any of the other original apostles. Then Paul, through the revelation of God, explained this *secret* in about 51 A.D. at the Jerusalem Council to the other apostles.

This *great secret* Paul described is the forthcoming wedding of the Jesus to His Bride, the Church which has been rehearsed on Rosh Hashanah for thousands of years by the Jews. Rosh Hashanah is the wedding rehearsal for the *taking away of the chosen bride (the Jewish people)*. The day is named *Mikraw Kodesh* in Hebrew, which signifies a holy day for the rehearsal for a wedding. Therefore, Paul's message was received because the disciples knew of the teachings surrounding Rosh Hashanah.

The word Paul used for the Rapture was *rapiemur* which means *to seize* or *to snatch away*. In other words, those who are alive will not experience physical death. Both the dead believers and those alive will meet Jesus in the air. This whole transformation will take place *"in a moment, in the twinkling of an eye."* In other words, it occurs instantaneously.

This first return of Jesus to Earth is an entirely different event from His Second Coming to save Israel and the nations at the end of the Tribulation. In the first return after His resurrection, the Lord will meet the body of Christ in the clouds. This is the Rapture, the *"blessed hope"* the body of Christ is expecting.

> *"[17]Then we who are alive and remain will be caught up together with them in the clouds to meet the Lord in the air, and so we shall always be with the Lord." (1 Thessalonians 4:17 NASB)*

> *"[13]looking for the blessed hope and the appearing of the glory of our great God and Savior, Christ Jesus." (Titus 2:13 NASB)*

In His *Second Coming*, the Lord returns to Earth and sets foot upon it.

> *"[4]In that day His feet will stand on the Mount of Olives, which is in front of Jerusalem on the east; and the Mount of Olives will be split in its middle from east to west by a very large valley, so that half of the mountain will move*

toward the north and the other half toward the south." (Zechariah 14:4 NASB)

The Church continues experiencing persecution during this present age before the Rapture.

"[12]Yes, and all who desire to live godly in Christ Jesus will suffer persecution. [13]But evil men and impostors will grow worse and worse, deceiving and being deceived." (2 Timothy 3:12-13)

God's master plan does not include the earthly presence of the Church during the seven years of Tribulation. The Church will be Raptured or removed from the earth because the Christian believers have the power to restrain Satan. It is necessary for God to remove them so He can display His power and wrath for the Jewish people as well as the non-believing Gentiles to convince them He is God.

Who is the bride in the wedding?

One of the ways in which God assures His people of His love for them is to describe Himself as their husband.

"[5]For your Maker is your husband, The Lord of hosts is His name." (Isaiah 54:5)

In the Old Testament, Israel can be compared to an unfaithful spouse, who commits spiritual adultery by worshiping false gods and forsaking the Lord. Therefore, God used the analogy of divorce to indicate how He felt about Israel.

"[8]Then I saw that for all the causes for which backsliding Israel had committed adultery, I had put her away and gave her a certificate of divorce." (Jeremiah 3:8)

God continues the analogy of husband and wife into the New Testament. The Bible uses imagery and symbolism of marriage to portray Jesus as the bridegroom and all believers in Jesus as the bride or *Church*. Numerous verses describe the relationship on earth between Jesus and His followers to be like a couple that is engaged to be married. Jesus is the bridegroom and each believer (male or female) is referred to as the bride (John 3:29). Jesus, the bridegroom, has sacrificially and lovingly chosen the church to be His bride (Ephesians 5:25-27).

> *"31For this reason, a man shall leave his father and mother and be joined to his wife, and the two shall become one flesh 32This is a great mystery, but I speak concerning Christ and the church." (Ephesians 5:31-32)*

Jewish wedding customs in the day of Jesus required the bridegroom to negotiate a price from the father of the bride. After a price was agreed upon, a binding contract was sealed by both parties by drinking a cup of wine. The bridegroom would then depart for about one year to go and prepare the home for his bride. This process signified the couple were *betrothed*, which is like our engagement process. Unlike the Jewish *betrothal* which was a binding marital contract and could be broken only through divorce, engagements today are not binding contracts of marriage.

Jesus drew up the wedding contract, which is an offer to everyone for the forgiveness of sin and eternal life, and they can accept or reject the offer. He paid the bridal price with His life by shedding His blood as an atonement for our sins.

Our process of entering into God's marriage contract begins when each individual believer places his or her faith in Jesus as Savior. The dowry paid to the bridegroom's parent (God the Father) would be the blood of Jesus shed on the Bride's (our) behalf. When a person places their faith in Jesus, they are *betrothed* to Jesus. They have entered the marriage contract (the New Covenant) and are part of the Church.

Jesus is now at His Father's house preparing the bridal chamber. The Apostle John describes it.

> "^{1}Let not your heart be troubled; you believe in God, believe also in Me. ^{2}In My Father's house are many mansions (dwelling places); if it were not so, I would have told you. I go to prepare a place for you. ^{3}And if I go and prepare a place for you, I will come again and receive you to Myself; that where I am, there you may be also." (John 14:1-3)

There was a *betrothal* period in Biblical times during which the bride and groom were separated until the wedding. All believers in the *Church* are brides enduring a similar separation from our Bridegroom, Jesus. All believers regardless of their church denomination comprise *The Church*.

Here are some of the verses that represent this relationship between Jesus and the believers in the Church.

Jesus called Himself the bridegroom:

> "^{15}And Jesus said to them, Can the friends of the bridegroom mourn as long as the bridegroom is with them? But the days will come when the bridegroom will be taken away from them, and then they will fast." (Matthew 9:15)

John called Jesus the bridegroom. The Greek word for *bridegroom* in all these passages is *numphios*, a newly married man:

> "^{29}He who has the bride is the bridegroom; but the friend of the bridegroom, who stands and hears him, rejoices greatly because of the bridegroom's voice. Therefore this joy of mine is fulfilled." (John 3:29)

Paul taught that Christians are now married to Christ.

> "[4]*Therefore, my brethren, you also have become dead to the law through the body of Christ, that you may be married to another - to Him who was raised from the dead, that we should bear fruit to God." (Romans 7:4)*

God provided us a similar wedding example in the Bible illustrating a simple and beautiful story that parallels our redemption by Jesus. The book of Ruth contains a story involving Naomi (a Jew), Ruth (a Gentile), and Boaz (the kinsman-redeemer). Boaz (representing Jesus) takes Ruth as his Gentile bride (representing the Church). After the marriage Naomi (representing Israel) is restored to her dead husband's land. This story starts as a tragedy, but evolves to become a beautiful love story with a great ending.

We can expect the same happy ending as believers when Jesus comes for us in the Rapture. Ultimately, many Jewish people experience the same happy ending of being united with their Messiah. Then they will be able to reclaim all the land promised to Abraham and live in peace.

Like the story of the ten virgins in Matthew 25, we should be watching and waiting for the appearance of the Bridegroom.

The Wedding

The Marriage Supper is the main event for every believer. It is mentioned only in Revelation.

> "[7]*Let us be glad and rejoice and give Him glory, for the marriage of the Lamb has come, and His wife has made herself ready. [8]And to her it was granted to be arrayed in fine linen, clean and bright, for the fine linen is the righteous acts of the saints. [9]Then he said to me, Write:*

> Blessed are those who are called to the <u>marriage supper of the Lamb</u>!" (Revelation 19:7-9)

The Biblical marriage described here is the consummation of the final event every born again believer should be looking forward to being a participant in – the completion of your earthly journey so you can be with Jesus throughout eternity.

While these verses are given near the end of Revelation, no indication is given if the event happens immediately after the Rapture, or near the end of the Tribulation before Jesus returns for the Battle of Armageddon. Since the chapter is near the end of Revelation, many Bible scholars believe it is the final event before they descend with Jesus to the Battle of Armageddon.

Who will participate in the marriage supper?

After the Rapture of the Church, there are only two groups of saints who have been resurrected at that time because they were part of the Rapture: the dead in Christ who were saved after Jesus was born and they accepted Him as their savior, and those believers alive at the time of the Rapture. During the Tribulation, the believers who will be beheaded or killed without taking the mark of the beast will also be resurrected (Revelation 20:4).

<u>None</u> of the Old Testament saints who lived *righteous lives* have been resurrected at this time. Therefore, they are not included in the Marriage Supper with the Lamb. Also, none of the righteous people from the Old Testament will return with Jesus as part of the army of heaven before the Battle of Armageddon (Revelation 19:14) since they have not been resurrected at that time. They will not be resurrected until the 1,000 years are completed.

> [4] And I saw thrones, and they sat on them, and judgment was committed to them. Then I saw the souls of those

who had been beheaded for their witness to Jesus and for the word of God, who had not worshiped the beast or his image, and had not received his mark on their foreheads or on their hands. And they lived and reigned with Christ for a thousand years. <u>⁵But the rest of the dead did not live again until the thousand years were finished."</u> (Revelation 19:4-5)

The Old Testament taught life after death and that everyone who departed from this life went to a place of conscious existence (Job 14:13; Psalm 6:5, Isaiah 38:10). The general term for this place was *Sheol*, which could be translated *"the grave"* or *"the realm of the dead."* Both righteous and wicked people reside there who will be called from Sheol to the Great White Throne Judgment.

The best description of what happens to both the Old Testament righteous and ungodly people is the story of Lazarus and the rich man in Luke 16:19-31. The rich man lived a life of extreme luxury while outside the gate of his house was an extremely poor man named Lazarus. The rich man was not concerned about the welfare of Lazarus. Eventually, they both died.

Lazarus went to the heaven side of Sheol, and the rich man went to the Hades side. A great gulf separates those in paradise from those in Hades. The rich man made a request that Lazarus be sent to cool his tongue with a drop of water to lessen his *"agony in this fire."* The rich man also asked Abraham to send Lazarus back to earth to warn his brothers to repent so that they would never join him in Hades. Both requests were denied. This story illustrates good rewards and punishments are immediate upon death.

Today, the transition to our eternal destination takes place the moment we die.

> "*⁴²Then he said to Jesus, Lord, remember me when You come into Your kingdom. ⁴³And Jesus said to him, Assuredly, I say to you, today you will be with Me in Paradise." (Luke 23:42-43)*

When believers die, they are immediately in the conscious fellowship and joys of heaven. When unbelievers die, they are just as immediately in the conscious pain, suffering, and torment of Hades. The rich man knew he was in Hades, and he knew why. He was eternally separated from God, and Abraham made it clear to him that there was no hope of ever mitigating his pain, suffering, or sorrow. Those in Hades will remember all the missed opportunities for salvation and their rejection of the gospel.

The story of the ten virgins should give believers the encouragement needed to keep watching for the bridegroom. We don't want to miss the Rapture when Jesus comes to take away His bride, the Church. I don't want to be around for the Tribulation.

Many scriptures indicate the believers will be spared God's wrath during the Tribulation. Here are two key verses making it inconsistent for God to promise believers that they will not suffer wrath, but then leave them on earth to suffer during the Tribulation.

> *"For God did not appoint us to suffer wrath but to receive salvation through our Lord Jesus Christ."*
> *(1 Thessalonians 5:9)*

> *"Because you have kept My command to persevere, I also will keep you from the hour of trial which shall come upon the whole world, to test those who dwell on the earth." (Revelation 3:10)*

After the Rapture of the Church, the Tribulation begins.

One more event involving believers who have either died prior to the Rapture and those who go up in the Rapture will be discussed in the next chapter.

Chapter 14

Judgment Seat of Christ or Bema Seat Judgment

What is the Bema Seat Judgment?

The Judgment Seat of Christ is also known as the *Bema Seat*. The words Bema Seat are not found in the Bible. The concept of the Bema Seat comes from the ancient Olympics. A judge would sit on the Bema Seat at the finish line to determine the position of the runners as they arrived at the finish line. They were given awards for finishing first, second, third, and so on. This is the imagery behind what is known as the *Bema Seat Judgment*.

> *"[10]But why do you judge your brother? Or why do you show contempt for your brother? For we shall all stand before the judgment seat of Christ. [11]For it is written:*
>
> *As I live, says the Lord, Every knee shall bow to Me, And every tongue shall confess to God. [12]So then each of us shall give account of himself to God." (Romans 14:10-12)*
>
> *"[10]For we must all appear before the judgment seat of Christ, that each one may receive the things done in the body, according to what he has done, whether good or bad." (2 Corinthians 5:10)*

In context, it is clear that both passages refer to Christians, not unbelievers. The judgment seat of Christ, therefore, involves believers giving an account of their lives to Christ.

Some scholars debate as to the exact timing of the Bema Seat. Some understand it to occur at the moment of death for each believer. Others believe the Bema Seat to occur right after the Rapture and all believers will be experience the Bema Seat judgment then. It is far more important to be prepared for the Bema Seat than to worry when it will happen.

The judgment seat of Christ does not determine salvation; that was determined by Christ's sacrifice on our behalf and our confession of belief in Him (John 3:16). All of our sins are forgiven, and we will never be condemned for them.

We should not look at the judgment seat of Christ as God judging our sins, but rather as God rewarding us for our lives. The apostle Paul described the process:

> *"[12] Now if anyone builds on this foundation with gold, silver, precious stones, wood, hay, straw, [13] each one's work will become clear; for the Day will declare it, because it will be revealed by fire; and the fire will test each one's work, of what sort it is. [14] If anyone's work which he has built on it endures, he will receive a reward. [15] If anyone's work is burned, he will suffer loss; but he himself will be saved, yet so as through fire."* (1 Corinthians 3:12-15)

Works of lasting value to the Lord will survive: the *"gold, silver, and precious stones."* Believers will receive crowns for different things based on how faithfully they served Christ (1 Corinthians 9:4-27).

Do not confuse the Bema Seat with the Great White Throne judgment which will be discussed in a later chapter.

Chapter 15

How and When the Tribulation Starts

Before the twenty one judgments in Revelation begin to unfold, a cataclysmic event must occur to produce a seven year peace agreement between Israel and its Islamic neighbors. Since its inception as a nation in 1948, numerous efforts to forge a peace plan between Israel and their Arab neighbors have failed.

In book one, *How and When the World Ends*, the rationale for Russia and the Arab countries desiring to attack Israel were described in detail. This summary does not include much of the information pertaining to the background of this war, but it has to be discussed because it has a huge impact on the people of Israel and the Tribulation.

The war that probably triggers the Rapture is described in Ezekiel 38 and 39. It is commonly referred to as the Ezekiel 38 War. The Rapture happens either right before or immediately after the war.

The details of this war were written over 2,500 years ago and it is the only instance in the Bible where the names of the countries are spelled out in advance of a war. Iran, Syria, Libya, and Russia come together to attack Israel, and Ezekiel declares the war only lasts one day.

Israel's victory in this war encourages the Jews that God has won the day and glorified Himself as He did in ancient times against Pharaoh (Ezekiel 38:23). They will believe God has intervened for them since they are His chosen people. They will celebrate the Fall feasts in glorious fashion. The Jews are euphoric and miss the significance of the Rapture and the multitudes of people who have vanished.

The world (including Israel's allies) will be severely traumatized by this war (Ezekiel 39:6), which will probably involve the use of nuclear weapons. Ending a war in one day with four nations will require the use of a dramatic weapon like an atomic bomb(s).

The Arab nations and Russia will be in shock and total defeat. Most people will doubt a peace plan can be achieved quickly because all previous attempts failed due to the major differences between Israel and Arab nations. The major stumbling blocks to peace has been the control of Jerusalem and the Dome of the Rock. The Muslim nations desire Jerusalem to be their capitol and they believe that Muhammad's Night Journey to heaven started from the rock at the center of the Dome of the Rock. The Dome sits upon the site where the next Temple will be built, so Israel wants it.

The Antichrist will have evolved to be the head of probably the European Union. Immediately after the war, he will successfully negotiate a seven year peace treaty with Israel. The Jews will be *ecstatic*.

The Rapture will occur either right before or right after the Jews defeat their enemies. The Tribulation will start immediately after the Rapture.

The Jews will not understand the Rapture and will develop a false sense of security in the next three and one half years.

Their joy will last only until the middle of the Tribulation when the time of *Jacob's Troubles* begin.

One question that has perplexed Bible scholars is "how long after the Rapture before this peace accord is signed?" Many think it will be several years so they have a gap of time between the Rapture and the start of the Tribulation. I don't believe there will be a gap of more than one or two weeks. It may be ten days of less because there are ten days between Rosh Hashanah and Yom Kippur.

Here is a comparison illustrating how quickly a peace plan can be developed when the victor has powerful weapons capable of mass destruction that are *locked and loaded* ready to be unleashed to deliver another devasting blow(s).

After the United States dropped an atom bomb on Hiroshima on August 6, 1945 and Nagasaki on August 9, 1945, Japan began negotiations to surrender on August 10. A decision was made to let all of the allies participate in the signing, so the treaty was signed on September 2, 1945 after 27 days. If it were not for this delay, the treaty could probably be signed in less than ten days. Also, don't forget in 1945 they did not have computers with word processors and the internet to make changes to the documents quickly.

The seven year peace plan will enable Israel to escape the first half of the Tribulation without experiencing additional wars. While the rest of the world will experience war, Israel will have peace.

When the *abomination of desolation* occurs in the middle of the Tribulation, the Jews' entire religious system is destroyed and taken over by the Antichrist. He will demand the Jews worship him as God, but they will refuse. Intense persecution follows, and the Jews will flee. All Jews are not only fleeing for their lives, but they begin searching for God, but not Jesus. They will lose all hope and experience death.

The Jews must proclaim Jesus as their Messiah for the Kingdom of God to come.

Here is additional information not widely taught today because it is rooted in the Old Testament.

The Kingdom of God coming to earth is contingent upon Israel's repentance. God is sovereign over all matters, and His universal kingdom extends over everyone. But, the arrival of the Millennial Kingdom on earth will not occur until Israel and the Jews turn from sin and accept Jesus as their Messiah.

> *"[6]O house of Israel, can I not do with you as this potter? says the Lord. Look, as the clay is in the potter's hand, so are you in My hand, O house of Israel! [7]The instant I speak concerning a nation and concerning a kingdom, to pluck up, to pull down, and to destroy it, [8]if that nation against whom I have spoken turns from its evil, I will relent of the disaster that I thought to bring upon it. [9]And the instant I speak concerning a nation and concerning a kingdom, to build and to plant it, [10]if it does evil in My sight so that it does not obey My voice, then I will relent concerning the good with which I said I would benefit it." (Jeremiah 18:6-10)*

The concept of Israel's repentance is repeated in these additional scriptures.

> *"[1]If you will return, O Israel, says the Lord, Return to Me; And if you will put away your abominations out of My sight, Then you shall not be moved. [2]And you shall swear, The Lord lives, In truth, in judgment, and in righteousness." (Jeremiah 4:1-2)*

This scripture reaffirms the truth that Israel will bless all the nations of the earth.

> "[2]I will make you a great nation; I will bless you and make your name great; And you shall be a blessing. [3]I will bless those who bless you, And I will curse him who curses you; And in you all the families of the earth shall be blessed." (Genesis 12:2–3)

> "[18]In your seed all the nations of the earth shall be blessed, because you have obeyed My voice." (Genesis 22:18)

These scriptures are critical to the final ending of the Tribulation when the Jews turn back to God by repenting of their sins and declaring Jesus to be their Messiah.

The Second Coming of Jesus at the End of the Tribulation

The Rapture will be on Rosh Hashanah. The Tribulation will end on Rosh Hashanah seven years later. Jewish Rabbinic literature states Rosh Hashanah is the anniversary of creation of the world; it is the day of judgment, and it is a day of renewing of the bond between God and Israel. The Jews believe that God created the heavens and the earth on this day. But most importantly, it is the day of the coming of their Messiah. This day is referred to as *The Second Coming of Jesus*.

The month of Elul precedes Rosh Hashanah. During this month the Jews pray and prepare for the Fall Levitical Feasts. The Jews will be in imminent danger of being eradicated from the earth since this is nearing the end of seven years of the Tribulation, the Jews will be praying fervently to God for deliverance.

The days preceding Rosh Hashanah not only are a special time dedicated to prayer, but they are also a time to remember sins and past wrongs. Jews seek forgiveness and turn their heart towards God before the Day of Atonement. Jewish custom states that if the people are faithful and cry out to God, then God will remember His chosen people and show mercy on the Day of Atonement or as it is called today, Yom Kippur. With their lives and very existence in jeopardy, the Jews will be earnestly praying for divine intervention on their behalf during this time.

What better day could God choose to send Jesus back to earth than one to save the Jews from imminent destruction? Rosh Hashanah!

The remnant of Israel - those who survive the final half of the Tribulation known as *Jacob's Trouble* - will see Jesus when He returns on Rosh Hashanah with His army of angels and saints. Then they have the opportunity to proclaim Jesus as their Messiah. When Jesus appears coming in His glory with the multitudes in His army, they:

> *"10look upon the One they pierced, repent of their sins, and receive Him as their Messiah." (Zechariah 12:10)*

The blast of a trumpet will announce the feast and the start of the new year, except this trumpet blast will signal the end of the current age and the arrival of the Millennium. The trumpet reminded the Jewish people of their past and of God's power. God is about to deliver His chosen people through a tremendous demonstration of His power.

God put hundreds of prophecies pertaining to the Second Coming of the Messiah in the Old Testament. Many require extensive study and the prophecies are interwoven with wars and invasions the nation of Israel experienced. However, several are very obvious as they describe the Second Coming of Jesus. They are included to make you aware God has a master plan and He wants everyone to know in advance His

Day of Wrath and judgment is coming. He also reassures Israel they will be saved from certain destruction.

Let's start with Joel and continue through several more prophets with the same message about the *end of the age*.

Joel:

> "*²I will also gather all nations, And bring them down to the Valley of Jehoshaphat; And I will enter into judgment with them there On account of My people, My heritage Israel, whom they have scattered among the nations; They have also divided up My land." (Joel 3:2)*

Isaiah:

> "*¹There shall come forth a Rod from the stem of Jesse, And a Branch shall grow out of his roots.*
>
> *⁴He shall strike the earth with the rod of His mouth, And with the breath of His lips He shall slay the wicked." (Isaiah 11:1, 4)*
>
> "*¹⁵For behold, the Lord will come with fire And with His chariots, like a whirlwind, To render His anger with fury, and His rebuke with flames of fire. ¹⁶For by fire and by His sword The Lord will judge all flesh; And the slain of the Lord shall be many." (Isaiah 66:15-16)*

Zephaniah:

> "*¹⁴The great day of the Lord is near; It is near and hastens quickly. The noise of the day of the Lord is bitter; There the mighty men shall cry out. ¹⁵That day is a day of wrath, A day of trouble and distress, A day of devastation and desolation, A day of darkness and gloominess, A day of clouds and thick darkness...*

> ...*[17]Because they have sinned against the Lord; Their blood shall be poured out like dust, And their flesh like refuse.*
>
> ...*[18]In the day of the Lord's wrath; But the whole land shall be devoured By the fire of His jealousy, For He will make speedy riddance Of all those who dwell in the land." (Zephaniah 1:14-15, 17-18)*

Zechariah:

> *"[15]The Lord of hosts will defend them; They shall devour and subdue with slingstones. They shall drink and roar as if with wine; They shall be filled with blood like basins, Like the corners of the altar.[16]The Lord their God will save them in that day." (Zechariah 9:15-16)*

Obadiah:

> *"[17]But on Mount Zion there shall be deliverance, And there shall be holiness; The house of Jacob shall possess their possessions." (Obadiah 17:1)*

If you continue reading through to verse 21, Obadiah describes how the house of Jacob repossesses their land when the *"Saviors shall come to Mount Zion"* (verse 21).

Micah:

> *"[12]I will surely assemble all of you, O Jacob, I will surely gather the remnant of Israel; I will put them together like sheep of the fold, Like a flock in the midst of their pasture; They shall make a loud noise because of so many people. [13]The one who breaks open will come up before them; They will break out, Pass through the gate, And go out by it; Their king will pass before them, with the Lord at their head." (Micah 2:12-13)*

Now for the Battle of Armageddon.

Chapter 16

The Battle of Armageddon and Judgment

The Battle of Armageddon refers to the final war between Satan, the Antichrist, human governments and God. The word *Armageddon* comes from a Hebrew word *Har-Magedone*, which means Mount Megiddo. The word *Armageddon* only appears once in the Bible in Revelation 16:16.

The exact location of the valley of Armageddon is unclear because there is no mountain called Megiddo. However, since *Har* can also mean hill, the most likely location is the hill country surrounding the plain of Megiddo, about sixty miles north of Jerusalem. More than two hundred battles have been fought in that region. The plain of Megiddo and the nearby plain of Esdraelon will be the focal point for the Battle of Armageddon.

The mention of the name Armageddon symbolizes the final conflict between God and the forces of evil in which God will intervene and destroy the armies of the Antichrist.

> *"[16]And they gathered them together to the place called in Hebrew, Armageddon." (Revelation 16:16)*

> *"[19]And I saw the beast, the kings of the earth, and their armies, gathered together to make war against Him who sat on the horse and against His army. [20]Then the beast was captured, and with him the false prophet who worked signs in his presence, by which he deceived those who*

> *received the mark of the beast and those who worshiped his image. These two were cast alive into the lake of fire burning with brimstone. [21]And the rest were killed with the sword which proceeded from the mouth of Him who sat on the horse. And all the birds were filled with their flesh." (Revelation 19:19-21)*

The Battle of Armageddon will bring humanity's 6,000 year reign on earth to an end. Daniel's prophecy of 70 weeks will be completed before Jesus establishes His reign in the Millennial Kingdom.

> *"[44]And in the days of these kings the God of heaven will set up a kingdom which shall never be destroyed; and the kingdom shall not be left to other people; it shall break in pieces and consume all these kingdoms, and it shall stand forever." (Daniel 2:44)*

Before Jesus returns, the opposing forces of Satan and the Antichrist will be gathered for Battle at Armageddon.

> *"[19]And I saw the beast, the kings of the earth, and their armies, gathered together to make war against Him who sat on the horse and against His army." (Revelation 19:19)*

The Apostle Paul disclosed the outcome of the Second Coming.

> *"[8]And then the lawless one will be revealed, whom the Lord will consume with the breath of His mouth and destroy with the brightness of His coming." (2 Thessalonians 2:8)*

Zechariah described it graphically.

> *"[12]And this shall be the plague with which the Lord will strike all the people who fought against Jerusalem: Their flesh shall dissolve while they stand on their feet, their*

*eyes shall dissolve in their sockets, And their tongues shall dissolve in their mouths. *¹³*It shall come to pass in that day hat a great panic from the Lord will be among them" (Zechariah 14:12-13)*

The Apostle John describes the ominous battle in this manner.

*"*¹¹*Now I saw heaven opened, and behold, a white horse. And He who sat on him was called Faithful and True, and in righteousness He judges and makes war. *¹²*His eyes were like a flame of fire, and on His head were many crowns. He had a name written that no one knew except Himself. *¹³*He was clothed with a robe dipped in blood, and His name is called The Word of God. *¹⁴*And the armies in heaven, clothed in fine linen, white and clean, followed Him on white horses. *¹⁵*Now out of His mouth goes a sharp sword, that with it He should strike the nations. And He Himself will rule them with a rod of iron. He Himself treads the winepress of the fierceness and wrath of Almighty God. *¹⁶*And He has on His robe and on His thigh a name written: KING OF KINGS AND LORD OF LORDS." (Revelation 19:11-16)*

Please Note: This white horse and rider is Jesus. The white horse and rider described in Revelation 6 is the Antichrist who is going out to conquer the nations by starting wars. Please remember: Satan always tries to imitate and make counterfeit God's way.

Do you remember the story of Jesus' final entry into Jerusalem when the crowds were hailing Him as their King? He rode on a donkey (Matthew 21:1-11), this time He arrives on a white horse. His eyes are like a flame of fires, on His head are many crowns, and His robe *"dipped in blood."* Not His own blood, but the blood of His enemies.

God used the prophet Isaiah to describe this very day in the following prophecy.

> "^{1}...This One who is glorious in His apparel, Traveling in the greatness of His strength? I who speak in righteousness, mighty to save.
>
> ^{2}Why is Your apparel red, And Your garments like one who treads in the winepress? ^{3}I have trodden the winepress alone, And from the peoples no one was with Me. For I have trodden them in My anger, And trampled them in My fury; Their blood is sprinkled upon My garments, And I have stained all My robes.
>
> ^{4}For the day of vengeance is in My heart, And the year of My redeemed has come.^{5}I looked, but there was no one to help, And I wondered That there was no one to uphold; Therefore My own arm brought salvation for Me; And My own fury, it sustained Me. ^{6}I have trodden down the peoples in My anger, Made them drunk in My fury, And brought down their strength to the earth." (Isaiah 63:1-6)

Isaiah is not describing Jesus' atonement on the Cross, for the Prophet adds *"For the day of vengeance is in My heart, And the year of My redeemed has come."* There was no *vengeance* in Jesus' heart on the Cross for He said *"Father forgive them for they know not what they do."* This is clearly a day of vengeance and salvation for humanity.

When the Jewish remnant see Jesus descending before the battle, they will recognize Him as their Messiah. Then repentance occurs, and salvation is obtained.

> "^{10}they look upon the One they pierced, repent of their sins, and receive Him as their Messiah." (Zechariah 12:10)

We do not know how God will use His power to win the battle. He will have at his disposal weapons including hail, earthquakes, flooding downpours of rain, fire and sulfur, lightning, and disease. Jesus' defeat of His enemies at this battle puts an end to the threat to Israel and by destroying the armies gathered against them which is the end of the Tribulation. The battle will be bloody, terrible, and result in complete victory for Jesus and the saints.

> *"[20]And the winepress was trampled outside the city, and blood came out of the winepress, up to the horses' bridles, for one thousand six hundred furlongs." (Revelation 14:20)*

The *"supper of the great God"* will be necessary to cleanse the land of all refuse from the Battle of Armageddon. The need of cleansing the land will be so great that the animal and fowl creations will be called upon to assist.

> *"[17]Then I saw an angel standing in the sun; and he cried with a loud voice, saying to all the birds that fly in the midst of heaven, Come and gather together for the supper of the great God, [18]that you may eat the flesh of kings, the flesh of captains, the flesh of mighty men, the flesh of horses and of those who sit on them, and the flesh of all people, free and slave, both small and great." (Revelation (19:17-21)*

The *"times of the Gentiles"* will be fulfilled.

Something often overlooked in discussing the Day of the Lord is that Jerusalem is set free of Gentile rule forever, or *"the times of the Gentiles"* is completed. Another Bible prophecy is fulfilled!

> *"[24]And they will fall by the edge of the sword, and be led away captive into all nations. And Jerusalem will be*

trampled by Gentiles until the times of the Gentiles are fulfilled." (Luke 24:21)

The times of the Gentiles refers to the period of time that began with the destruction of Jerusalem and Solomon's temple by Nebuchadnezzar and the Babylonians in 586 B.C.

The times of the Gentiles also includes the destruction of Jerusalem and the second temple by Titus and the Romans in 70 A.D. The times of the Gentiles further includes a future time during the last half of the Tribulation period when Jerusalem will be surrounded and conquered by Gentile armies.

"²But leave out the court which is outside the temple, and do not measure it, for it has been given to the Gentiles. And they will tread the holy city underfoot for forty-two months." (Revelation 11:2).

The times of the Gentiles ends with the Second Coming of Jesus when He defeats the Gentile armies led by the Antichrist at the Battle of Armageddon.

The Fulfillment of the Last Two Feasts: The Day of Atonement (Yom Kippur) and Tabernacles

The last trumpet of Rosh Hashanah will signal the start of a brief span of fifteen days preceding the start of the 1,000 year Millennium. The Day of Atonement will come after ten days, and the Feast of Tabernacles will occur five days later.

The Jewish survivors from the Tribulation will be rejoicing over their deliverance from certain death, but also over the coming of their Messiah. They will begin preparing for Yom Kippur by repenting of their sins so they will come into right standing with God before Yom Kippur. An ancient Jewish belief about Yom Kippur calls for it to be celebrated as the day of salvation for the nation of Israel. This is another Jewish Feast and teaching that will come to fruition! Israel and its people will be free from oppression and their salvation will be complete.

The Day of Atonement or Yom Kippur will also be a time of great rejoicing in heaven. Israel and the Jewish people will repent of their sins and proclaim Jesus as their Messiah.

Sadly, it is also the day of judgment for all non-believers.

The Judgment of the Sheep and Goats On the Day of Atonement

The sheep and goat judgment of Matthew 25 on the Day of Atonement is the day King Jesus judges individual survivors of the Tribulation. This judgment determines who enters the Millennial Kingdom. Note that this judgment is for only people who are alive at the end of the Tribulation.

> "^{31}When the Son of Man comes in His glory, and all the holy angels with Him, then He will sit on the throne of His glory. ^{32}All the nations will be gathered before Him, and He will separate them one from another, as a shepherd divides his sheep from the goats. ^{33}And He will set the sheep on His right hand, but the goats on the left." (Matthew 25:31-33)

Believers who physically survive (never die) the Tribulation period are called sheep and will enter the Millennial Kingdom. Jesus heaps praise on these believers for their actions for their belief in Him as their Savior.

> "^{34}Then the King will say to those on His right hand, Come, you blessed of My Father, inherit the kingdom prepared for you from the foundation of the world: ^{35}for I was hungry and you gave Me food; I was thirsty and you gave Me drink; I was a stranger and you took Me in; ^{36}I

> *was naked and you clothed Me; I was sick and you visited Me; I was in prison and you came to Me.*
>
> *[37] Then the righteous will answer Him, saying, Lord, when did we see You hungry and feed You, or thirsty and give You drink? [38] When did we see You a stranger and take You in, or naked and clothe You? [39] Or when did we see You sick, or in prison, and come to You? [40] And the King will answer and say to them, Assuredly, I say to you, inasmuch as you did it to one of the least of these My brethren, you did it to Me." (Matthew 25:34-39)*

Since it is the Jews who were most tormented during the last half of the Tribulation, Jesus will commend the actions of those believers on His right hand for caring for starving Jews by giving them food and drink, for providing shelter to those fleeing for refusing to take the mark of the beast, 666, for clothing those that were naked, and visiting them when they were sick and in prison.

He said to the non-believers, or goats:

> *"[41] Then He will also say to those on the left hand, Depart from Me, you cursed, into the everlasting fire prepared for the devil and his angels: [42] for I was hungry and you gave Me no food; I was thirsty and you gave Me no drink; [43] I was a stranger and you did not take Me in, naked and you did not clothe Me, sick and in prison and you did not visit Me.*
>
> *[44] Then they also will answer Him, saying, Lord, when did we see You hungry or thirsty or a stranger or naked or sick or in prison, and did not minister to You? [45] Then He will answer them, saying, Assuredly, I say to you, inasmuch as you did not do it to one of the least of these, you did not do it to Me [46] And these will go away into*

everlasting punishment, but the righteous into eternal life." (Matthew 25:41-43)

This judgment ensures *no* unbelievers go into the Millennium. Please remember, the believers who are alive at the end of the Tribulation enter into the Millennium in their physical earthly bodies and continue to live, marry, and have children. They will repopulate the earth. Children will be born into the world as non-believers and will have to make the decision to accept Jesus as Lord and Savior like their parents did. However, Satan will be bound so they will not have Satan present tempting them like we do in this age.

Some people will not accept Jesus as their Savior, therefore, there will be non-believers who are alive at the end of the Millennium. They will go to The Great White Throne Judgment (Revelation 20:11–15).

The Feast of Tabernacles follows five days later after The Judgment of the Sheep and Goats which was on the Day of Atonement or Yom Kippur. Tabernacles can be translated as *Festival of the Ingathering* or *Harvest Festival*, or the *Festival of Booths.* The Jewish feasts are closely related to Israel's spring and fall crop harvests. The Spring feast was celebrated on the Feast of Weeks or Pentecost, and the Fall feast on Tabernacles. The Spring feast was a smaller harvest than the much larger Fall harvest.

God's plan of salvation corresponds to these two annual harvests celebrated in ancient Israel. God's plan for redeeming humanity into the Kingdom of God follows the same harvest plan.

The small Spring harvest of first fruits occurred when Peter preached to the 3,000 on Pentecost. The people who accepted

Jesus as their Savior became the firstfruits of salvation with the indwelling of the Holy Spirit.

At this post-Tribulation Feast of Tabernacles, the number of believers will be greatly enlarged because of the millions upon millions of people who were Raptured and the millions of people martyred in the Tribulation. They will all come together for one glorious feast!

God wanted the ancient Israelites to overflow with joyfulness, thanksgiving and rejoicing during the Feast of Tabernacles. This celebration will be extremely joyful, full of thanksgiving and praise.

> "[13]You shall observe the Feast of Tabernacles seven days, when you have gathered from your threshing floor and from your winepress. [14]And you shall rejoice in your feast." (Deuteronomy 16:13-14)

> "[16]and the Feast of Harvest, the firstfruits of your labors which you have sown in the field; and the Feast of Ingathering at the end of the year, when you have gathered in the fruit of your labors from the field." (Exodus 23:16)

The celebration of the Feast of Tabernacles completes all seven of the Jewish feasts exactly as rehearsed by the Jewish people for thousands of years!

Now it is time to enter into the Millennium.

Chapter 17

Conclusion

The Millennium

The Millennium is the name given to the thousand years Jesus will rule over the whole earth from Jerusalem.

It is going to be a truly amazing time on earth. The entire earth will be ruled by Jesus, His bride, and the martyred saints (Revelation 20:4).

Several more unconditional promises which God made to Abraham, King David, and the nation of Israel will be completed in the Millennium. The Promised Land will be fully restored to Israel, the nation will prosper and become the greatest nation on earth, the people will live in peace, and the Tabernacle of David will be rebuilt.

At the end of the Millennium, Satan will be loosed from his chains for a short time, though it is unclear exactly how long this time is. Satan will gather an army from all over the earth and they will surround Jerusalem again. God will then send fire down from Heaven to devour them. The devil will finally be cast into the lake of fire and brimstone where the Beast and the Antichrist are, and they will be tormented there forever (Revelation 20:7-10).

The Last Judgment

At The Great White Throne judgment, every person from past ages plus those alive at the end the Millennium will be judged. This final judgment occurs at the end of the Millennium before Eternity begins.

Everyone who has died will now be resurrected and together with the living, they will be judged. Books are opened which contain all the details of what everyone has done in their life. Another book is opened called the Book of Life.

> "*[11]Then I saw a great white throne and Him who sat on it, from whose face the earth and the heaven fled away. And there was found no place for them. [12]And I saw the dead, small and great, standing before God, and books were opened. And another book was opened, which is the Book of Life. And the dead were judged according to their works, by the things which were written in the books. [13]The sea gave up the dead who were in it, and Death and Hades delivered up the dead who were in them. And they were judged, each one according to his works. [14]Then Death and Hades were cast into the lake of fire. This is the second death. [15]And anyone not found written in the Book of Life was cast into the lake of fire." (Revelation 20:11-12).*

All who practiced unrighteousness, in any of its forms, and remain unrepentant, receive God's wrath and righteous judgment, regardless of who they are or their religious background. All whose name is not found written in the Book of Life will be cast into the lake of fire. Those with their names recorded in the Book of Life will enter into Eternity with all the other believers.

"⁶And He said to me, It is done! I am the Alpha and the Omega, the Beginning and the End. I will give of the fountain of the water of life freely to him who thirsts. ⁷He who overcomes shall inherit all things, and I will be his God and he shall be My son. ⁸But the cowardly, unbelieving, abominable, murderers, sexually immoral, sorcerers, idolaters, and all liars shall have their part in the lake which burns with fire and brimstone, which is the second death." (Revelation 21:6-8)

Eternity

When God makes everything new, that includes even a New Heaven and a New Earth, because both the old Heaven and the old Earth have been tainted by sin.

Keep the faith, live in HOPE and be blessed.

If you have enjoyed this book, please consider being kind enough to give it a good review. To give a review, go to amazon.com, enter *Revelation and Daniel Reveal How and When the World Ends*, then scroll down to Customer Reviews, and click on Write a customer review. If you have never given a review, you can simply state you enjoyed the book and recommend it.

The next book in this End of World series, *Heaven, Millennium, and Eternity* Volume 5 describes our glorious future. It describes how God completes His remaining unconditional promises and describes our lives in God's coming Kingdoms. Learn about the changing environments and roles the saints experience as they transition from one eternal place to the next. The overriding theme of this book is HOPE for believers to live in peace from now to Eternity.

Please consider reading these other books in this series:

How and When the World Ends, Volume 1. Analyzing Jewish idioms and Jesus' words reveal the day of the Rapture and when the Tribulation and End Times start.

End Time Rapture Signs: How and When the World Ends, Volume 2. Learn how to recognize End Time signs, and have hope during these stressing times.

The Date of the Rapture: How and When the World Ends, Volume 3. A probable date of the Rapture and alternative dates are presented.

Concluding Thoughts

God allows humanity to exercise their free will to accept or reject Jesus, but each of us is responsible for our own choice. Love is a uniquely human trait God created in us which can be overwhelmed by unforgiveness, bitterness, and hate.

Jesus Christ, who came and dwelt on Earth as God in the flesh, exemplified the passion and love of God for us. On the evening before Jesus faced a cruel scourging and death by crucifixion, He reflected on the ultimate love from a human perspective, *"Greater love has no one than this, than to lay down one's life for his friends"* (John 15:13).

Since Jesus led a sinless life, He did not have to die. *"For the wages of sin is death, but the gift of God is eternal life in Christ Jesus our Lord"* (Romans 6:23). Jesus decided to take the death penalty for our sins.

You have a free will to reject God and Jesus, which makes you a non-believer. However, this state can be changed and you can live in love, peace, and harmony with God. God's heart is that He *"is patient toward us, not willing that any should perish but that all should come to repentance"* (2 Peter 3:9).

For those that have accepted Jesus Christ as Savior, His promise is that He will never leave us. *"And surely I am with you always, even until the very end of the age"* (Matthew 28:20).

He also promises that, whenever we stray from *"good"* (being in God's presence) to *"evil,"* (by turning away from God), He is faithful to find and restore those who have turned away or became lost like a prodigal son (Luke 15:11-32).

And for those who have yet to find Him, God's promise is that He is desperately searching for you. *"For the Son of Man came to seek and to save what was lost"* (Luke 19:10).

Many millions have been deceived in their thinking. They believe they are a good person, and God's love and mercy will wipe away their sins so they can go into eternity and live happily ever after. God deals with sin through grace with forgiveness for those who repent. But it is Jesus who is going to judge the unrepentant sinner and non-believer (*"good people"* included) and sentence them to eternal damnation in the lake of fire.

Many people fear death, the Rapture, or the Tribulation horrors. Believers do not have to fear death because Father God is preparing a dwelling place for us to live forever. We are commanded to be *"looking forward to the new heavens and new earth where righteousness dwells"* (2 Peter 3:13). The new Heaven and Earth are our future and eternal home.

Are you a believer in Jesus and have been *"born again?"*

Being born again means you believe Jesus is the Son of God, and you ask God to forgive your sins. The love and happiness you long for comes with reconciliation to God, which causes joy to flow into your soul. This lasting joy comes when you accept by faith Jesus Christ as your Lord and Savior and live a life dedicated to Him.

Because God loves you, He always seeks to be with you. *"Here I am! I stand at the door and knock. If anyone hears my voice and opens the door, I will come in and eat with him, and he with me"* (Revelation 3:20). To experience unbelievable love and forgiveness, simply open the door and ask Jesus to come into your heart.

I would be remiss if I did not ask you this question:

If after reading all these horrible End Time events that are coming, *have you made the commitment to accept Jesus as your Savior by turning away of your sins and asking Him to come into your life as your Savior?*

If not, please pray to God and ask that your sins be forgiven. Ask Jesus to come into your heart and save you. Then live for Him. Study His ways and follow His commands to *"love God and love people."*

It is as simple as that. It also enables you to escape with the Church at the Rapture, and you will avoid going through the Tribulation. Your life will be filled with hope!

If you prayed this prayer, I encourage you to find a local church you can call your *"home"* church to strengthen you in your walk with God, Jesus, and the Holy Spirit.

A Thank You From The Author

Dear reader,

It is with sincere gratitude that I would like to thank you for reading *Revelation and Daniel Reveal How and When the World Ends.* We are living in trying and difficult times. I hope this book has provided you with peace and comfort. Keep watching at Rosh Hashanah every year!

If you have enjoyed this book, please consider being kind enough to give it a good review. To give a review, go to *amazon.com*, enter *Revelation and Daniel Reveal How and When the World Ends,* then scroll down to Customer Reviews, and click on *Write a customer review.*

You can contact me at: erbrist@gmail.com

May God greatly bless you and keep you safe!

Earl Bristow

Glossary of Terms

Antichrist can be a person or force who opposes God's Kingdom. The Antichrist is represented in Daniel and Revelation as the beast ten horns representing ten kings who comprise heading an evil empire battling against God. In the middle of the Tribulation, the Antichrist will destroy the harlot's religion. When the Antichrist declares he is God, then he probably takes control of his mind and body.

Apocalypse in biblical terms speaks of the return of Jesus to rescue His people. For non-believers and society in general, the apocalypse has come to mean the complete and final destruction of the world.

Beast of Sea or Another Beast comes out of the sea and is symbolic of the false prophet who is only called another beast once. Every other time he is called the false prophet.

Believer in Christ (or Jesus), *saved* and *born* again have interchangeable meanings in this book. The definitions vary by denomination, so I am going to keep this simple and apply the following descriptions to each of these words. Any person who acknowledges and believes in their heart:

- God is the Father, Jesus Christ is the Son of God, and the Holy Spirit are one triune being.

- Jesus is the sacrificial Lamb of God who chose to die on the cross to atone for our sins so we could be in right standing with God the Father.

- After Jesus died, He rose from the dead, descended into Hades, then ascended into Heaven where He resides at the right hand of God the Father.

- Jesus will return to Earth to unite with all believers who have died and those who are alive. He will judge the non-believers.

Bride (of Christ) is a believer in Christ and is also a part of the Church.

Bridegroom is a term used to represent Jesus.

Church refers to all people worldwide who believe Jesus is the Son of God.

The dragon is always symbolic of Satan.

First beast is symbolic of the Antichrist and comes out of the earth in Revelation. In Daniel the first beast was also symbolic of King Nebuchadnezzar.

First Coming is the thirty-three years of Jesus' birth, life, death, and resurrection on Earth approximately 2,000 years ago. Jesus ascended into Heaven to complete His First Coming.

Gentile is any person who is not Jewish.

Great Harlot or Harlot of Babylon is the term used throughout the Bible as a metaphor for false religion. The harlot is neither the Antichrist nor the false prophet. The harlot refers to another person, possibly persons, in charge of this religious institution.

Little horn is the *little horn* that rises from the head of the terrifying beast in Daniel 7:8. The little horn represents the Antichrist in future time when the Antichrist establishes and controls a one-world religious system through the false prophet.

Rapture is the event when Jesus will appear in the sky above the Earth and summon up to Him in Heaven all the dead who believed in Him and all the true believers actively in a relationship with Jesus who are alive on Earth. His appearance at this time is *not* His Second Coming.

The word Rapture evolved from the Latin word *rapiemur.* The word harpazo in the Greek has the same meaning. The word *harpazo* means to seize, to snatch, to catch up or to carry away. The use of the word Rapture has become a popular and correct replacement for the phrase *"caught up."*

The purpose of the Rapture is to save the church, or body of Christ, from the wrath of God that comes during the seven years of Tribulation. Jesus will not be visible to the non-believers when He returns. The impact of millions of people instantly vanishing into the air will have a profound impact on those left behind. The Rapture triggers the start of the Tribulation.

Seven heads are seven empires from history that persecuted Israel: Egypt, Assyria, Babylon, Persia, Greece, Rome, and the revived Roman Empire.

Ten horns represent a future ten nation confederation of ten kings that rule simultaneously together under the Antichrist's authority. The common belief is these nations will come of the European Union (EU), or they will take over the E.U.

Tanakh is an acronym of the first Hebrew letter of each of the three traditional subdivisions of the Torah (*'Teaching,'* also known as the *Five Books of Moses*), Nevi'im (*'Prophets'*) and Ketuvim (*'Writings'*) therefore, the name TaNaKh.

Torah, Talmud, Mishnah – The **Torah** is the Hebrew Bible, and while some people think of just the Five Books of Moses *Torah* refers to all the Hebrew Bible, including such books as Joshua, Psalms, Book of Ruth, etc. ... The **Talmud** is the compilation of the historic rabbis *"discussing"* or *"debating"* what the *Torah* means.

Talmud is Hebrew for *"learning,"* appropriate for a text that people devote their lives to studying and mastering.

Mishnah is the main text of the Talmud, a collection of teachings written in Hebrew, redacted by Rabbi Yehuda the Prince, in the years following the destruction of the Second Temple in Jerusalem in 70 A.D.

Tribulation is a future seven-year period beginning either immediately or a short time after the Rapture. Since the Rapture has taken all the true believers from the Earth, the remaining people on Earth do not believe in Jesus. At this time, God initiates a series of plagues bringing death and destruction in hopes the non-believers will repent and turn to Him. The Tribulation is often referred to as the *"Time of Jacob's Troubles"* because of the unparalleled amount of suffering the Jewish people endure for the rejection of their Messiah, Jesus.

Satan was created as one of the cherubims and held a position of great authority. God possibly placed him in charge of all creation since he was in the Garden of Eden. Satan was cast out of heaven because of his sin (Ezekiel 28:11-16). Satan's downfall came from his pride by declaring he would ascend into heaven and exalt his throne above the stars of God (Isaiah 14:13).

Through deceit and trickery he caused Eve to eat of the forbidden fruit. This brought sin into the world of humanity.

Currently, Satan is *"the prince of the power of the air"* (Ephesians 2:2) and has a vast host of demons (Matthew 7:22) committed to him. Satan has the power of death upon earth (Hebrews 2:14). He still has access to God as the *"accuser of our brothers"* (Revelation 12:10) and continues to bring sin and wickedness into the world.

At the beginning of the Great Tribulation Satan's access to God as accuser will be withdrawn and Satan is removed from Heaven. Satan turns his attention to the earth and wreaks havoc during the last half of the Tribulation primarily on the Jews. At the Battle of Armageddon, Satan and his demons are defeated and cast into the Lake of Fire for 1,000 years. At the end of the 1,000 years he is released for a short while, and is defeated again. He is then cast forever into the Lake of Fire

Second Coming of Jesus refers to the instance where Jesus physically returns to Earth after the seven years of Tribulation have been completed. He physically steps onto the Mount of Olives and is seen by all. The Second Coming is described as *"The Day of Lord"* in the Bible, which is a dark day of judgment for the non-believers. *"That day is a day of wrath, A day of trouble and distress, A day of devastation and desolation, A day of darkness and gloominess, A day of clouds and thick darkness." (Zephaniah 1:15)*

A war (Armageddon) like the world has never experienced occurs on this dark day. Jesus comes the second time as the warrior King of Kings and the Lord of Lords. He destroys the enemies of Israel, establishes His Kingdom, and begins His 1,000 year reign on this Earth.

Wedding, Divorce, and Marriage

God instructed the writers of the Bible to use terminology, imagery, metaphors, and similes to aid understanding of His instructions. One of the most prominent Bible metaphors in both the Old and New Testaments is the Jewish wedding process. The Old Testament comparison is a man and a woman entering an engagement and marriage. This marriage is similar to the relationship between the nation of Israel and God. Because of its unfaithfulness, God rejects and divorces Israel. Jeremiah describes the divorce:

> *"Then I saw that for all the causes for which backsliding Israel had committed adultery,* **I had put her away and**

given her a certificate of divorce; *yet her treacherous sister Judah did not fear, but went and played the harlot also." (Jeremiah 3:8)*

The New Testament metaphor describes in detail the pending wedding of the bridegroom, Jesus, to His bride, the Church. God terminated (divorced) the relationship with Israel when Jesus became the sacrifice for our sins, which ended the Old Testament Jewish laws. Every person, including all Jews who fail to enter the marriage contract with Jesus, faces eternal consequences.

Bibliography

It is important to note I do not endorse all the content in these books or websites. It is equally important to note they **DO NOT** endorse the work in my book either. Below are books and web sites relevant to this book.

All Jewish Feast days were taken from this calendar:

http://www.cgsf.org/dbeattie/calendar/?roman=32https://www.christianpost.com/news/5-notable-failed-end-times-prophecies.html

Web Sites:

https://bible.org/seriespage/12-abrahamic-covenant-and-premillennialism

https://www.chosenpeople.com/site/the-biblical-boundaries-israel/

https://doctrine.org/understanding-the-book-of-revelation

https://www.crosswalk.com/church/pastors-or-leadership/ask-roger/is-the-battle-of-armageddon-around-the-corner.html

https://www.gotquestions.org/millennial-kingdom.html

https://www.bibletools.org/index.cfm/fuseaction/Topical.show/RTD/CGG/ID/7075/Fullness-of-Gentiles.htm

https://www.blueletterbible.org/faq/don_stewart/don_stewart_151.cfm

https://israelmyglory.org/article/tabernacles-in-the-millennium/

https://www.ministrymaker.com/four-beasts-of-revelation

http://www.askelm.com/star/star014.htm

https://www.endtime.com/blog/times-of-the-gentiles-fulfilled/

http://endtimepilgrim.org/70wks8.htm

https://www.biblestudytools.com/commentaries/revelation/related-topics/ten-tribes-lost.html

https://www.LifeHopeandTruth.com

https://saintsunscripted.com/faith-and-beliefs/laws-and-ordinances/bible-say-no-marriage-after-death/

http://www.biblicaltruths.com/gods-plan-mankind/

https://www.biblestudytools.com/commentaries/revelation/related-topics/who-populates-the-millennial-kingdom.html

Books:

Tim LaHaye, No Fear of the Storm, (Multnomah, Sisters, OR: 1992, pp. 51-57)

Mordechai, Avi Ben, *Signs in the Heavens*, Millennium 7000 Communications

Morris, Henry, *The Revelation Record*, Wheaton, Illinois, Tyndale House, and Creation Life

Conner, Kevin, *The Feasts of Israel,* Bible Temple Publishing, Portland, Oregon 97213

Dake, Finis, *Dake's Annotated Reference Bible,* Dake Bible Sales, Inc., Lawrenceville, Georgia 30245 (Permission granted to use various commentaries.)

Printed in Great Britain
by Amazon